SECRETS

OF THE

MIRACLE

INSIDE

SECRETS OF THE MIRACLE INSIDE

FIND WHAT'S MISSING TO MAKE YOUR LIFE INCREDIBLY GOOD

PAUL McCORMICK

MIRACLE WRITERS, LLC
– PUBLISHING COMPANY–

Copyright © 2007 by Paul B. McCormick

Published by:	Miracle Writers LLC Publishing Company RCM #28550 P.O. Box 4120 Portland, Oregon 97208-4120 United States www.MiracleWriters.com
Cover Design:	George Foster Foster Covers
Book Design:	Rachael Costner Sands Costner & Associates
Copy Editor:	Val Dumond Muddy Puddle Press

The author of this book does not prescribe any treatments or offer any medical advice or recommend any of the techniques in this book be used as a form for emotional or spiritual treatment without the advice of a physician. The information provided is intended to offer only general information related to your search for emotional and spiritual well being. The author and the publisher assume no responsibility for your actions.

Library of Congress Cataloging-in-Publication Data

McCormick, Paul, B.
   Secrets of the Miracle Inside
   ISBN-13: 978-0-9794338-3-2
   ISBN-10: 0-9794338-3-5
   LCCN 2007902330

10 09 08 07 06 05 04 03 02 01
First Printing, May 2007

Printed in the United States of America

CONTENTS

I Love You
Nicole
and
Brandon

Acknowledgments

This book might never have been written if it were not for my family that brought me to the place I am today. During my darkest hour when I felt overwhelmed with life and wanted it to end, it was the love of my wife and son that kept me alive.

I thank my wife for enduring seventeen years while I searched to find myself. During all that time she remained steadfast and full of love and commitment. I thank my son for coming into my life at the perfect time and for being a catalyst to shatter my illusion that life outside of me could be peace, love, joy, or happiness.

My family brought about the events and life experiences necessary for me to shed the illusion and see life for what it is: perfect, lovely, and full of joy, abundant in every way.

Preface

This book shows how to find what's missing in life, and how to fill your life with peace, happiness, love, good health, wealth, and purpose. If you are like me, then despite the successes in your life, you always knew something was missing to make life more satisfying.

Searching to find satisfaction is like searching for something in the night when you are only able to see shadows. You reach for something, but it turns out not to be what you wanted. In your search for satisfaction you may have pursued a career, success, love, religion, or money, but all these things produced only short-term satisfaction. They were only a counterfeit of something you still hoped could be found.

Perhaps you have experienced a long time of pain and suffering even while you searched for peace in your life. You wanted to become free of your pain, but no matter how much you tried to forget, you couldn't. The memories of hurt and pain continued.

Maybe you spent your early adult life chasing money as a way to find happiness, only later to realize you did not find what you were looking for. You may have started the search all over again, still hoping to find an answer. You might have divorced your spouse, changed careers, joined the athletic club, lost weight, created a new hair style, found a new companion, or changed religions. Like the early years, these changes may have brought happiness for a while; but then you came to realize something was still missing.

Not knowing where to look or what to look for is the worst part about the search for happiness and fulfillment. Everything you've tried has failed to provide lasting happiness, and maybe you've even lost hope that an answer exists. It is no accident you're here, now, reading this.

An answer does exist. The way to find it has remained a secret, hidden from you. This book shows where and how to find the secret. The secret is not new. It has been around for as long as people have existed. What you will find is a miracle that will transform your life forever.

This book is not about religion, getting rich quick, or about motivational psychology. It is about learning to find a secret hidden inside you, showing how to connect with a power that will transform your life forever. When you find this secret, you will find:

+ Happiness
+ Contentment
+ Peace
+ Security
+ Prosperity
+ Purpose
+ Connection to Source

+ Freedom
+ Good Health
+ Energy in Life
+ Excitement
+ Riches
+ Heaven on Earth
+ Miracles Every Day

The miracle you will find is that you can connect with your Source, and it is *inside you*. You are a part of it. Some people call this Source *God* or *Spirit* or *Consciousness*. Most of these names produce a limited and misleading view of the true nature of your Source. When you find the secret inside, you find the miracle leading to happiness and peace forever. You find your own ability to create yourself and the world around you as you desire it to be. Your effectiveness in accomplishing this depends only upon you learning how to connect with the Source inside you.

The miracle remains a secret hidden from most people because they don't know where to look. They seek all the things that are *outside* themselves, looking in the wrong places. The secret remains locked inside, waiting to be found. The answer has always been inside you. That is why it begs you to find it.

This book shows how to find that secret. It gives you the steps to find the miracle inside, and shows how to use what you find to bring about the life you desire.

"When you change the way you look at things,
the things you look at change."

Dr. Wayne W. Dyer

You perceive who you are

through your thoughts.

If you change your thoughts,

do you change who you are?

Introduction

Why I Wrote this Book

This book is not about my life or my life experiences. However, in this introduction I offer a glimpse into my life so you will understand how I struggled and eventually came to discover the secrets of the miracle inside me.

I was an ordinary person who struggled in the same ways you might be struggling. For more than thirty years my life was ordinary, although it became increasingly difficult for me to cope. Eventually, I experienced such emotional pain I wished for my life to end. But through that pain, I came to find the secret inside me that showed me the way to achieve complete happiness, peace, and freedom — forever.

My life is no longer ordinary; it is *extra-ordinary*. Today I'm thirty-eight years old, excited, energetic, free, peaceful, healthy, and wealthy. I have peace about everything that happens, despite what happens all around me or to me. I am in control of my life circumstances and my feelings. I absolutely love life. You can too.

When you find the secret and learn how to use it, there is no limit to what you can do or how happy and peaceful you can become. Money, fame, success, or love is not what brings happiness or freedom; if you seek those things, you will never find lasting happiness. You first must seek the miracle inside. When you find that miracle, everything you desire can become yours.

My life was not always amazing and wonderful. The following words describe my life during my early years.

Ordinary	*Pain*	*Judgmental*
Unworthy	*Fear*	*Low Self-Esteem*
Poor	*Hatred*	*Angry*
Lonely	*Wanted to Die*	*Selfish*
Sad	*Self-Conscious*	*Self-Centered*

I was born, raised, and still live in the Puget Sound region of Washington State. My parents raised my two sisters and me to believe in strong Christian values, which worked in my life for about thirty years. In some ways, growing up, I felt very ordinary. But in most ways I felt less than ordinary. I was raised in an ultra-conservative Christian environment where we were taught life-styles that were very different from others. My religion taught it was a sin to: own a television, wear makeup or jewelry, attend movies, play cards, smoke cigarettes, drink alcohol, listen to non-Christian music, swear, or even to say "gee-whiz."

My sisters and I went to public schools and integrated the best we could without being tainted by all the "sinners." In elementary school I was an average student, but I had difficultly reading so I was put in special education classes for five years until I became "average" in reading. I wanted to become accepted by those around me, yet I could not go to parties like all the other kids or even join their cliques. Instead, I worked hard to excel in academics; by high school I had become a straight-A student. While I was never one of the popular kids, I was well-known and liked by most of my peers because of my academic success.

When I was fourteen, my parents decided to move to a more mainstream church. Until then I had been taught to believe that the world of rules and religion was printed in black and white. I had learned that our lifestyle was "right" and others were "living in sin." This move to a new church allowed me to see that real people who also searched for spirituality existed beyond the limits of my original understanding.

I chose to attend college because I grew up with the unquestioned assumption that I would become an engineer like my father. I received a tuition scholarship to attend the local community college and worked summers in order to graduate from the University of Washington with a degree in engineering. The Monday after graduation I started work in my new career. Three months later I married the woman I'd been dating for six years.

Emotional Struggles in Career

I still wanted to be accepted by people around me. Subconsciously, I harbored a huge void in my life because I grew up not feeling loved, despite the love my parents gave me. When I started working, I pursued career success as a way to fill the void in my life. I did not know what my life was missing, but I thought it was the feeling of being valued. I pursued money and attention as a way to achieve it. For the next ten years I sacrificed everything in my life in order to succeed in my career, assuming that would translate into financial success and prove I was valuable and worthy.

My commitment to work put me in the position of becoming a partner in the firm at age twenty-seven and CEO at twenty-nine. The firm grew and prospered, and I believed I was the driving force behind its success. That did not make me feel any better; in fact it made me feel worse, because attaining success proved to do nothing to solve the problems in my life. I had chased "success" to get rich and become valued which, I thought, would eliminate my painful memories of not being loved. However, no amount of success or money could change this. I was in a position guaranteed to fail. I became resentful toward my business partners because I saw them as the problem, holding back financial reward and appreciation which I thought would be the answer to my problem.

My disappointment grew to resentment, bitterness and anger. I wanted to run from my problems, so I contemplated resigning. But, I had no place to go, so in disappointment I stayed. I hated my work and my life.

Emotional Struggles in Family

During this same time, I saw my five-year-old child feeling his own pain, realizing he was different from other children. Our doctors and other specialists labeled him with several medical terms that describe neurological conditions, one of which was Autism. These conditions do not define who my child is, but rather define conditions of the mind and body that we learn to live with. Only now is it clear that our son came to us at the perfect time to challenge our ideals, our will power, our faith, and our love. His life helped to break down my ego-based ideals, my beliefs in an external God, and to build unconditional love toward him, others, and myself.

At the time, I struggled to understand it all, and was angry at God for allowing this difficult time. My son's pre-school teachers were not adequately trained to understand the special needs of high-functioning children with neurological challenges. The formal education experience eroded his self-esteem. As I saw my son become depressed, I dropped further into my own depression as my wife and I struggled with how best to help him.

Struggles with Failing Health

During this time I experienced chronic fatigue which made it difficult to get through each day. I never quit my job; but many nights by the time I got home I collapsed on the bed, and other times I walked through the front door and lay down on the carpet because I was too tired to walk to the bedroom.

In an attempt to improve my health, I forced myself to start running every day, hoping that exercise would help my energy level and my health. I also tried to ride my bike to work as much as possible. One day while riding my bike home from work, the fender broke, jamming the front wheel. I crashed, landing on my head, was knocked unconscious, and ended up in the hospital. A CAT scan proved no damage, but showed a chronic sinus infection; the doctor put me on antibiotics for ten weeks.

Six weeks into the ten-week dose, I became very ill with

clostridia difficile, which occurs when the good bacteria in the intestine are destroyed by the antibiotic and the bad bacteria take over. It can kill you if not treated. With proper medication I soon recovered. For the second time in six weeks I was forced to lie down for several days, away from work. There I reflected on my miserable life as it seemed to get worse each day.

Four weeks later I was back to running hard, trying to build good health to fight off the chronic fatigue. Then I hurt my leg badly; an MRI scan turned up a stress fracture in the top of my femur bone, and I was told I would lose my hip socket unless I stopped using that leg for two months. Here was the third major health issue I faced within a two-month period; every part of my life was getting worse. I was physically weak, angry at people I had to work with, and confused spiritually. I had been praying to God for years to help me and my family. For all those years nothing changed.

Emotional Suffering from Loss of Faith

At the same time I was being bombarded with stress at work, stress at home, and stress in my physical body, my struggle extended to my faith in God. Despite the fact that I had always had a strong faith and relationship with God, I felt that I no longer found God in my life. I stopped believing in a God who would allow the suffering and pain I was experiencing. I had been taught God would never allow more pain than someone could bear; but there I was and I could not bear it. I stopped believing in a personal God. I wanted to die so badly, I thought often about ways to end my life.

I don't know what kept me alive, but somewhere inside I still hoped to find what I knew was missing from my life. I still hoped to connect with something bigger than me, to make everything better. For the first time in my life, I read about Eastern religions, occults, pagan religions, and witchcraft as another way to search for divine help. Absolutely nothing helped and nothing answered my prayers. That search lasted for two years.

I stopped looking and gave up hope. I had abandoned all my Christian beliefs and any belief in God. I was devoid of belief in anything; I simply knew I hurt very bad.

What I Found

After I stopped looking for an answer, I found the secret. Something prompted me to look inside myself. Up until then, everything I had sought was outside myself: religion, career, money, love, and affection. But, inside me was an area I had never searched. I read about people who found the connection to where they came from, inside themselves.

By reading about the experiences of others, I learned *how* to look inside myself, and there I found a miracle. I found my connection to where I came from. It was a *connection* to my Source, the place from where I came. It was not just a connection to something bigger than me. Rather, it *was* me; I *was* a part of it.

Some people call what I found "God." That word implies something separate from me. The idea of a separate God is what I was taught when I was young; this no longer made any sense to me.

What I found was not anything like a personal God. What I found is difficult to explain in mere words. It is a state of becoming one with the Source of everything. This Source can be described as:

All knowing
Existing in me
Existing in you
Total love
Complete peace
Unlimited compassion
Responsible for everything
Existing inside all creation
You cannot exist without it
Total intelligence
Being all places at once
It cannot exist without you
Eternal, no beginning, no end
All power and energy of the universe
You are part of it
I am a part of it

I found inside myself a state of becoming connected with this Source of everything, the energy of everything, the love and peace of everything. You may call it a connection, but it is better stated as becoming *one* with it. The problem with the word *God* is that it has come to mean a supreme being. That idea is misleading because there is no "being;" *there is only the Source.*

The Source is not a person, not a being, not in one place. The Source is unlimited consciousness with intelligence, but not residing in any form. The Source is not personal and not judgmental, and not selective about anyone or anyone's behavior. The Source is unlimited energy existing in all places at the same time, living inside people, animals, rocks, trees, wind, and ocean. Experiencing the Source is a state of not just feeling and knowing complete love, but of actually *being* complete love. When you connect with it you experience total peace and complete power.

Call this life force "God" or "Spirit" or "Source" or whatever you choose. I use "Source" with the definition above, because it is the Source of everything and has no negative religious connotations.

The secret is that you can find this inside yourself.
The miracle is that you are a part of it; it is a part of you.

In essence, you are already a part of this "Source," even if you are not yet aware of it. The miracle is gaining the awareness to see that you are a part of this "Source." These days I describe my life with the following words.

Free
Loving life
Happy
Compassion
Worthy
Feeling good
Peaceful
Money is unlimited
Energetic
One with my Source
Love self
Transcend all pain
Healthy
Enjoy everything
Secure
Have fun

This book shows how to find what I found. It shows where to look and how to use this discovery once you find it.

My passion is to teach what I've learned to those who are struggling, as I was, to find what is missing from life. If the answer was not hidden, everyone would have found it. It's your turn to find the way.

Here are what I call the **Ten Steps to Finding the Secret Inside**. Here is how you can find what I found.

Ten Steps to Finding the Secret Inside

1. Understand your current perception
2. Heal your emotional pain
3. Look inside yourself
4. Choose new beliefs
5. Live in the present
6. Find creative power within you
7. Be emotionally aware
8. Align your personality
9. Embrace what "Is"
10. Transcend the illusion

Each step is explained in the following chapters. Most people grow up believing things are one way when in fact things are not the way they appear to be. Misleading beliefs result in dissatisfaction and pain. These ten steps show how to see the world in a different light, offering you a way to produce peace, happiness, and good fortune. When you understand how things really are, then you will see that things really are all good.

You perceive who you are
through your thoughts.

If you change your thoughts,
do you change who you are?

<u>CHAPTER I</u>

Understand Your Current Perception

This chapter shows how you have come to view everything the way you do. This is *Step One* in the **Ten Steps to Finding the Secret Inside**.

Ten Steps to Finding the Secret Inside

1. *Understand your current perception*
2. Heal your emotional pain
3. Look inside yourself
4. Choose new beliefs
5. Live in the present
6. Find creative power within you
7. Be emotionally aware
8. Align your personality
9. Embrace what "Is"
10. Transcend the illusion

While growing up, people form beliefs about themselves and about the world. Those beliefs may be inaccurate, causing distortion of how the truth looks. Think about the beliefs you formed as a child and recall how you developed them. Most likely, the beliefs you formed before you were eight years old are the same ones you still hold today. Those beliefs influence exactly how you view yourself and the world around you.

Child Development

You began forming your personality while you were still in your mother's womb. In the womb you perceived your experience as neutral, neither good nor bad because there was no other experience. While you were inside the womb you felt warm and wet. You lived with constant pressure on all sides of your body to keep you confined to a curled-up position. You would not like living like that today for nine minutes, let alone nine months. It was fine then because you had nothing else to compare it to.

While you were small, your experiences provided the input necessary for you to gather, process, and store information about the world around you.

Eventually, you began to make judgments and decide things you liked and didn't like. In contrast, remember the fetus forming in the womb; experiences are neutral. By the time you were a two-year-old, you had thousands of experiences to use as comparisons; you were able to form judgments about what you liked and didn't like. A negative thought triggered a negative emotion; you remembered this. A positive thought triggered a positive emotion which you also remembered.

During the first several years of your life, many thousands

of thoughts and emotions were stored in either your conscious or subconscious mind. All those memories and emotions became layers to your personality, making you unique from any other person. Each memory influenced your future perceptions.

Here's an example: If you were picked up as a baby and spoken to loudly, you might not have liked it. Remember, all experiences are neutral. Still, you perceived it as negative. You had just come from nine months living in the quietness of the womb. Living outside the womb, loud sounds felt unpleasant. When you heard someone speak loudly, you compared it with the quietness you had been used to and decided you didn't like the loud voice. The result was to feel bad or angry about it. Your bad feeling was stored in your memory to influence future events in your life. When you were picked up again, you may have automatically recalled the memory of the bad feeling and cried. Whatever new experience you would have with this sound or this person would be influenced by the memory of the past experience.

In this way, you formed layers to your personality, the layers of who you think you are. You stored all your likes and dislikes, your joys and fears, all of which shaped your character, your thoughts, your emotions and your memories. These are the things that make you different from anyone else. You and your siblings experienced the exact same childhood environment, but you each formed different personalities because you had different thoughts and feelings about those life experiences. During your childhood you developed fears of things as simple as the noise in the example above.

A common emotion is the basic fear of not being loved; it affects millions of people. Any number of experiences could have triggered this initial emotion. All life experiences are neutral, but you don't perceive them as neutral if you have a preconceived idea about what the experience should be like.

At one time in your childhood you likely experienced feeling unloved. One time might have been when a parent became upset with you. When this happened, you formed an emotional response of fear that your parent was disappointed, unhappy, and didn't love you at the moment. Whatever the feeling, once it was formed it began to influence the way you saw things the next time they happened. The feeling could also influence other situations for the rest of your life. Most of the time you have no idea you feel this way, because it is buried inside the subconscious mind.

Fear may influence your self-esteem for many years. After the fear-causing event you might perceive any number of neutral experiences in life as negative, resulting in a subconscious view of yourself as unloved and unworthy of being loved.

Over time more bad experiences support the fear of not being worthy of love. The many layers to your personality continue to pile up. You might have learned to compensate by hiding this emotion. You might have acted as if you didn't need love, or pretended you really were loved. But inside, there remained the fear and sorrow that have been familiars emotion to you for a long time.

Stored emotions are so powerful that they continue to influence the quality of your life as an adult. You have read the example of the fear of not being loved. But you may have other emotions buried inside you. These buried emotions influence the way you see yourself and the world, supporting the negative thoughts and causing you to feel the same pain you felt as a child.

While today's experiences are neutral, they do not feel neutral; they feel painful. Perhaps the experiences of today are different, and the places and people are different, but the emotions are the same ones that have brought pain to you all your life.

Perception of Yourself

As an adult, you have perceptions about who you are, based on your personality, your likes and dislikes, memories, and emotions. Most people base their view of life on how life looks. But people who know the secret realize that you must first change the way you see life in order for life to change.

As a child, you did not know you could control how things look by controlling your beliefs. So when you saw the world, you accepted it "as is." You did not realize it only looked that way because that was how you already believed it to be. The same is true with yourself.

You perceived yourself to be a certain way based on how you felt and what people said about you, and you accepted it as the truth. You did not realize it only looked that way because that was how you already believed it to be. If you would have changed the way you believed about yourself, you would have actually become changed to match what you believed yourself to be. But, you kept looking at your situations as bleak and so they stayed bleak.

People confuse the situations around them as being part of who they are rather than being temporary. You hear people saying these things about themselves:

+ I am a Catholic
+ I am a professor
+ I am an American

+ I am a Muslim
+ I am a politician
+ I am an actor
+ I am a photographer
+ I am an artist
+ I am a writer
+ I am married
+ I am a college graduate
+ I am a business owner

Or you may hear things people say about other people:

+ She is Caucasian
+ He is tall
+ She is aloof
+ He is rich
+ She is a Republican
+ He is autistic
+ She is smart
+ He is poor
+ She is clumsy
+ He is handsome

These labels are not who you are or who anyone else is. These are descriptions of temporary conditions, not to be confused with who you really are. You might see yourself as a list of labels that have been given to you by others. Your list is based on your accomplishments, your failures, your appearance, your heritage, and all the labels people have given you as you grew up.

These labels limit you from seeing who you really are: a

divine being connected with your Source and able to accomplish anything.

What Is Your Personality?

For a moment, pretend you can step outside your body and stand beside it. While outside your body, look at your personality. It is a collection of thoughts about yourself that you've been storing since you were born. It includes all the feelings which you have saved since the day you were born. Make these two observations:

1. Your personality did not exist until you formed it in your mind. You were very young when you formed your view of self, based on limited knowledge and experience. Now that you are older, consider changing that view.

2. The personality you formed demands a lot from you.
    a. Your personality holds grudges.
    b. Your personality never forgets past hurts.
    c. Your personality remembers bad times better than good times.
    d. Your personality retains memories that imply you are weak, unloved, and unworthy.
    e. Your personality worries about the future.
    f. Your personality fears not getting what it wants.
    g. Your personality needs to be loved to be fulfilled.
    h. Your personality needs to be accepted.
    i. Your personality needs to feel worthy.
    j. Your personality needs to perform and get acceptance.
    k. Your personality causes you to hurt.

Your personality is full of baggage from past experiences. It causes hurt based on perceptions that might not even be true. Now that you are learning who you really are and how much power you have (to change everything based on what you decide to believe), you might consider changing your personality to designate with who you want to be rather than with who you think you are.

*All pain comes
from one false belief,
that you are separate
from your Source.*

CHAPTER 2

Heal Your Emotional Pain

This chapter shows how to heal yourself from emotional pain. This is *Step Two* of the **Ten Steps to Finding the Secret Inside**.

Ten Steps to Finding the Secret Inside

1. Understand your current perception
2. *Heal your emotional pain*
3. Look inside yourself
4. Choose new beliefs
5. Live in the present
6. Find creative power within you
7. Be emotionally aware
8. Align your personality
9. Embrace what "Is"
10. Transcend the illusion

What You Believe Is What You See

Your beliefs influence how you see yourself, how you see the world around you, and how you feel about everything. Positive beliefs cause you to see the world as a wonderful place. Negative beliefs cause you to see the world as a difficult place. Your beliefs determine which world you see.

Positive beliefs help you see a world filled with love where only the things that are supposed to happen do happen. Only good comes to you; you never experience misfortune and pain, and everything is exactly as it should be. You are happy and at peace no matter what anyone says or does to you. All circumstances of your life have purpose and good meaning; because of this, you embrace everything happening to you.

Negative beliefs cause you to see a world where circumstances appear out of your control, bringing pain and suffering. You see misfortune, death, disease, hunger, and injustice. When you believe the things that allow you to see the world in this way, you feel pain, and life is filled with struggles and difficulties. The more you focus on these things the more you see the ills of the world and the more obstacles come your way.

The beliefs you choose influence how you feel. Life's experiences are neutral; they are neither positive nor negative. But you pass judgment on those experiences anyway and label them as positive or negative depending upon your beliefs.

Your beliefs are what make you think things should be a certain way and not another way. For example, if you believe there exist good and evil in the world, then you assign certain things as "good" and certain things as "evil." The universe does not create labels of good and evil; you do.

You make decisions about which activities in life you engage in and which ones you do not engage in based on how you label them. Once you believe that the world contains both good and evil, you will see both good and evil in it.

You will see everything the world displays according to your beliefs. The world will appear to support your beliefs and provide proof that good and evil exist. But, the world really only provides neutral circumstances which you have chosen to call "good" or "evil" because of your naiveté in seeing the bigger picture. When you make judgments, you choose to influence your view of the world and you will feel either *good* or *bad* because of it.

Negative Beliefs Cause Suffering

When you believe a negative belief, it brings pain and suffering. For example, if you believe God is something separate from yourself, you expect the universe to be a certain way. You approach life with a preconceived idea about how things should be in the world. You expect God to intervene when things get difficult. You expect to hear and receive guidance for your life. Then when life gets hard and no outside assistance appears, you feel abandoned. You might be hurt and become angry or bitter toward God; you feel bad.

This is how a negative belief brings pain. If you never believed God to be separate from you in the first place, then God could never abandon you, and you would never be able to experience that sort of pain. You could not be angry at God for allowing suffering in the world if you had not first believed there is a being called *God* that is allowing all that suffering in the world.

All negative beliefs bring pain because you establish

expectations about the world being a certain way based on that belief. When the world does not operate your way, then you become hurt, or upset, or angry. Shouldn't your suffering point you in the direction of changing your belief so you no longer believe thoughts that bring pain?

Personal Revelation

One day while sitting on an airplane I realized why all my life I had been driven to achieve such a high level of success at the expense of my happiness. It was because I had a false belief about myself. I believed I could fix my childhood hurts by finding love and acceptance as an adult. I grew up feeling unworthy of love. I spent all my life striving to be better than everyone around me in an effort to make myself worthy of being loved.

It is silly to think that I can fix the hurt of my childhood by getting appreciation now. But that is how I lived my life every day for over thirty years. The past cannot be re-created; no matter what I do now, I cannot change the past.

As a child I felt hurt. My subconscious mind held onto that emotion to be recalled hundreds of times throughout my life. These stored memories became a part of me. These negative imprints defined me. They formed layers of my personality.

I carried the hurts for my entire life and was never conscious of them. I built my life around the false illusion of who I thought I was and on what I thought I needed to do to fix it. It caused me to pursue "being great" in an attempt to become worthy of being loved. I lived a shallow life because it was based on the illusion of who I thought I was rather than on the reality of who I was. So no matter what level of success I achieved, I never felt any better; I continued to hurt.

Breaking the Cycle

You too probably have buried emotions from childhood that hurt you, whether or not you are aware of it. These emotions manifest themselves by making you feel bad. Whatever the emotion, it is probably a recurring one that you have experienced many times over throughout your life. It controls your life without you knowing it, because it makes you continue to act in certain ways that cause you to feel bad.

Notice that while the circumstances might be different, the bad feeling is the same as it has been all your life. This indicates that the cause of the pain is one from a long time ago. Use the following Seven-Step Process to heal yourself. Whenever you feel emotional pain:

1. **Ask yourself if the emotional pain seems familiar.**
   a. Have you felt this same pain many times before? Even though the people and circumstances might be different, is this the same emotion you have felt all through your life?
   b. If it is, then acknowledge that the emotion is not a result of the current circumstances, but rather because of a hurt from childhood buried inside you.

2. **Find the childhood experiences which started the process.**
   a. When you recognize that the feeling is a recurring theme, turn your attention off of the current circumstance and look inward to find the hurt you felt in the past. Review your childhood memories and find the experiences that caused these feelings for the first time. Recall as many memories as you can that brought the same feeling. These

are all the experiences that helped you form a perception about yourself early in life.

3. **Find the belief you formed about yourself.**
   a. As you recall the memories that triggered the hurt feeling, think about what perception you formed about yourself as a result. Did you decide you were not good enough? Did you decide your parents did not love you? Did you decide you were unworthy of being loved? Did you decide you were worthless? What belief did you form?

4. **Realize that you don't want this belief to be true. You act the way you do because you want to change the memory of the hurt you experienced as a child.**
   a. When you find the belief you formed about yourself, ask how you feel about it. Does it make you feel bad? Do you wish it were not true?
   b. If, as a child, you believed you were unloved by a parent, then today you probably wish that were not true. If, as a child, you came to believe you were worthless, you probably don't want to believe you are worthless now. If, as a child, you believed you would never get things right in life and were never good enough, you probably wish it were no longer true.
   c. Do you find yourself trying to please people because you need their approval to prove you are good enough? Do you find yourself seeking relationships in an attempt to prove you are worthy of love? Do you seek to be great in order to prove you are worthy of attention? Do you serve others at your expense to prove you are worthy of their

affection? Do you try to control other people to prove you are somebody with power? Do you do whatever is necessary to be accepted by your peers to prove you are worthy of their love and acceptance?

    d. Even getting what you want today does not make you feel better because you still remember the hurt of your past; you keep believing the very thing you do not want to believe about yourself.

5. Choose a new belief.

    a. The original belief was formed by you as a child with limited knowledge and limited life experience. Recognize that it was a false belief. You don't want it to be true and it hurts you to believe it. Let this feeling be your guide directing you to change that belief.

    b. Now, as an adult, you are more capable to form healthier beliefs. If you don't like the belief you formed as a child, change it. You cannot change the memory of the pain, but you can change the truth about who you are today.

    c. Acknowledge that you were hurt as a child. As a child you did feel hurt, but you do not need to keep feeling hurt about it now. Recognize that you keep acting certain ways as an adult because you are trying to change the belief you formed as a child because you don't want it to be true.

    d. No matter what you do now, you cannot change the fact that as a child you did experience hurt in this way. Your actions today are useless in making that memory go away. You are trying to change the past, which is impossible. Accept what happened as a child, but choose now to stop it from continuing to be true or continuing to hurt you; don't let it remain a part of your life today.

e.   To change the belief, choose a new belief to replace the old one and repeat it to yourself every day. Then act on it daily.

6. **Change your actions and thoughts to align with your new belief.**

    a.   Stop acting and thinking in negative ways that support the false belief which only brings the hurt feeling.

    b.   When you find yourself acting in ways to fix the past or to prove the past belief to be wrong, stop yourself and acknowledge that you no longer need to fix the past since that is impossible to do anyway. You were hurt in the past only because you had a false belief about yourself. Act and think now in a way that is consistent with your new belief, and you will feel peace all the time.

7. **Choose to forgive and choose to love.**

    a.   Forgive God for allowing you to be hurt as a child, forgive the people who initiated it into your life, and forgive yourself for believing a lie for so long.

    b.   Love yourself for being who you are. Love yourself because you are worthy of being loved. Love yourself for being capable of healing yourself of this hurt, and for being able to find true love, peace, contentment, happiness, and freedom to make a new life just as you want.

Make a conscious decision to change how you think about yourself now and to change what you believe today. Accept that the lie you used to believe about yourself brought pain. While you might not be able to forget that, you can stop it from continuing to hurt you again. Recognize that your searching for peace has been based on a false childhood belief that you can change the past. Now that you know the truth, you have only two choices:

You can choose to be happy.
You can choose to be hurt because you were hurt in the past.

Below are some examples of people who have put this lesson into practice.

Sally's Story

Sally is married and has two children. She is intelligent, organized, and always busy serving others. She participates in volunteer parent organizations at school; she volunteers at church functions, family functions, and community functions. She is esteemed by everyone who knows her because she is a leader with talent to organize and get things accomplished.

She serves people constantly and wants to do this for people. On the surface she believes she finds joy in helping others. But, the happiness of helping others is short-lived. Most of the time, she is not happy. She keeps looking for ways to help others as a way of searching to fix a problem in her own life. She sacrifices her sleep, her free time, and her health in order to serve others. She knows something is missing in her life and she seeks the answer by serving others. Still, she never feels better. No matter how much good she does for others, the feeling she has about herself never changes. She is not happy and does not know how to be happy.

If your life is like Sally's, then use the Seven-Step Process to heal yourself.

1. **Ask yourself if the emotional pain is familiar.**
    a. Sally has always felt that she is never good enough, so she works to perform and never stops trying to become good enough. She has lived with this same feeling throughout her life.

2. **Find the childhood experiences that started the process.**
    a. Sally's parents were perfectionists and encouraged Sally to do things the *right* way. Whenever things were not perfect, her parents showed her how to do it the "correct" way.
    b. Sally can remember many times as a child when she felt hurt. No matter how hard she tried, she still did not get things perfect enough for her parents to accept.

3. **Find the belief you formed about yourself.**
    a. Early in life Sally developed the belief that she would never get it right the first time and that she simply was not good enough to receive people's approval.

4. **Realize that you don't want this belief to be true. You act the way you do because you want to change the memory of the hurt you experienced as a child.**
    a. Sally did not want to feel the way she did, so she decided to work harder to become better. She dedicated her life to becoming good at many things and in serving others to get approval.
    b. Sally's life has been shaped by her need to change the belief about herself that she does not want to be true. Her life has been spent trying to change that belief, but it never changes.

    c.   No matter how well she performs and how much others appreciate and praise her, she cannot erase the memory of pain. No matter what she does now, she still feels the same way inside: not good enough.

5.   **Choose a new belief.**

    a.   Sally has learned to see the falseness of her childhood belief. This belief brought pain then and will continue to bring pain as long as she continues to believe it. She has chosen to stop believing the lie of her past and has made new beliefs about who she wants to be. She wants to be good enough just the way she is, so she chooses to believe this is true.

6.   **Change your actions and thoughts to align with your new belief.**

    a.   Sally now takes time for herself. She does not feel the need to over-commit herself to serving others. She serves people only in areas that are most important to her. She now makes time to go on walks, play with her children, and use her creative talent.

7.   **Choose to forgive and choose to love.**

    a.   Sally forgives her parents for being perfectionists and for initiating those painful emotions into her life. She forgives God for allowing it to happen. Finally, she forgives herself for believing in the lie for so long.

    b.   She chooses to love herself and is able to laugh when she makes mistakes.

John's Story

John is married and has three children. For twenty years he has been working to advance his career. He has never been satisfied with his current status and has sacrificed his happiness, his health, and his family in order to advance his career.

Even though he has advanced his career significantly, he does not feel any more satisfied than he did when he started. His children will soon be leaving home and he feels as if he missed much time with them while they were growing up. He always believed life would get easier after the next promotion or the next big change in position, but it never did. John believes that he works at a slower pace than others and that things do not come as easily to him as they do for others. So he works long hours with much persistence to compensate for his perceived weakness.

John feels something is missing in his life to make him happy. He is driven to perform. Still, the harder he works, the more it takes him away from everything else important to him. The feeling of dissatisfaction only increases.

If your life is like John's, then use the Seven-Step Process to heal yourself.

1. **Ask yourself if the emotional pain is familiar.**
   a. John has always felt that he does not perform at a high enough level, whether in school, sports, work, speaking, or anything else. He frequently feels the same way about himself.

2. **Find the childhood experiences that started the process.**
   a. John's father had many interests but none of them included

John. As a child John remembers wanting to spend time with his father, but his father was busy with hobbies and other things besides John.

b. John tried to get his father's attention and affection by performing well, but it didn't work. John wanted praise or credit for the work he did, but it never happened.

3. **Find the belief you formed about yourself.**

a. John began to believe that he was not performing well enough, so he tried harder. After John left home, he no longer felt the need to get his father's attention, but he felt the need to be the best at everything he tried. John still felt it was not good enough.

4. **Learn how you don't want this belief to be true. You act the way you do because you want to change the memory of the hurt you experienced as a child.**

a. John wanted his father to accept him for who he was. John does not want to have to perform for approval. John does not like believing that he is under-performing and not worthy of love, because it hurts.

b. John sees that his workaholic nature is in response to his desire to be good enough to receive love. No matter how hard he works, the bad feeling never changes, even though he is successful at what he does. Even when others praise him, it only brings short-term satisfaction before the old hurt returns.

c. John sees that no matter how good he is at what he does, he cannot erase the memory of pain. As a child he did feel hurt. No matter how hard he works today, he will not be able to erase the memory of the pain. He can stop trying to accomplish the impossible.

5. **Choose a new belief.**
   a. John has chosen to believe he is good enough just the way he is. He recognized that his perception of not being good enough is a lie. He believes in being happy without the need of other people's approval to validate the belief. He finds value in himself without the need to perform.

6. **Change your actions and thoughts to align with your new belief.**
   a. John chooses to work a more normal work schedule and does not feel guilty for doing so. He enjoys evenings and weekends with his family and takes more vacations. He spends time exercising, eating better, and doing things he likes outside his career. He finds that his happiness has improved.

7. **Choose to forgive and choose to love.**
   a. John forgives his father for not giving him attention and for initiating those painful emotions into his life. He forgives God for allowing it to happen. He forgives himself for believing a lie about himself for so long.
   b. He chooses to love his life.

Dianne's Story

Dianne is a single mother. Because of her financial situation, her son lives with her half the time and with her parents the other half. Dianne married when she was eighteen years old, but the marriage lasted only one year. Her marketable skills are the ones she gained through numerous office clerical jobs. She struggles with low self-esteem and does not see herself able to get ahead financially.

As a teenager Dianne tried using drugs and alcohol to forget how bad she felt about herself and her life problems. She moved from relationship to relationship, but never found the love she hoped for. As an adult she struggled with low self-esteem and depression.

If your life is like Dianne, then use the Seven-Step Process to heal yourself.

1.   **Ask yourself if the emotional pain is familiar.**
     a.   Dianne has always felt unworthy of love and not as valuable as everyone else around her.

2.   **Find the childhood experiences that started the process.**
     a.   Dianne grew up with loving parents and a sister, but she knew that she had been adopted, and she always wondered why her birth parents did not keep her.

3.   **Find the belief you formed about yourself.**
     a.   As a child Dianne believed she was not worth being loved by her birth parents, and that is why they put her up for adoption.

4. **Realize that you don't want this belief to be true. You act the way you do because you want to change the memory of the hurt you experienced as a child.**

   a. Dianne always wanted to be loved by her birth parents and wishes they would have kept her because that would mean she was good enough to be loved. Even now Dianne wishes she could feel loved, but she cannot find that feeling.

   b. While growing up Dianne did whatever her friends did because she wanted them to like her, but she never felt accepted or loved in the way she needed.

   c. No matter what she does now she cannot remove the memory of pain that she had as a child.

5 **Choose a new belief.**

   a. Dianne has chosen to accept the memory of the childhood pain. She knows that as a child she hurt because she believed her adoption was a result of her unworthiness.

   b. As an adult she recognizes this might not be true at all and she chooses to believe her adoption is not related to her value. Since she wants to be worthy of love, she has chosen to believe that she is worthy of love.

6. **Change your actions and thoughts to align with your new belief.**

   a. Dianne, no longer seeks relationships to fill the void in her life. By no longer needing love, she is now able to love herself and give love to others. As a result she has found real love in a new relationship that is not based on the need to receive love, but on sharing love. She has found the first real love of her life.

b. Because she values herself, she is investing in herself to become better educated and equipped with the skills that will enable her to build a business.

7. **Choose to forgive and choose to love.**
   a. Dianne forgives the parents that put her up for adoption, and forgives God for allowing her to feel such pain. She also forgives herself for believing a lie about herself for such a long time.
   b. She loves herself and believes she is worthy of other people's love. Now that she knows how to love herself, she is able to give her son real love as well.

Simon's Story

Simon is married and has two children who are now grown and living on their own. He has always wanted to accomplish much more than he has been able to. He always dreamed of making a lot of money and being able to travel, able to give to those in need, and able to buy luxury homes and luxury cars. He envied those who were able to do these things.

He believed life was against him. Although he thought of business ventures that could be successful, he knew that he would never be able to make them successful and never took the risks.

As he came into mid-life, he felt unfulfilled. Something was missing in his life as it always had been; he believed it was the financial success he so deeply wanted but which eluded him. Now he believed he would never see it.

If your life is like Simon's, then use the Seven-Step Process to heal yourself.

1. **Ask yourself if the emotional pain is familiar.**

   a. Simon has always felt he would not be able to be as successful as the people around him. He perceived other people to be at the right place at the right time when he wasn't. He perceived others to have fast success in life, while he never did. While growing up, Simon felt sorry for himself. Now, he feels the same way again; this is the recurring emotion of pain.

2. **Find the childhood experiences that started the process.**

   a. Simon grew up in a home which valued hard work and earning a good wage for a good day's work. He was taught that money did not grow on trees and that he would have to work hard for his money.

3. **Find the belief you formed about yourself.**

   a. Simon developed a belief early in life that things would be hard for him and that life was not quite fair to him and that he would have to work hard for everything.

4. **Realize that you don't want this belief to be true. You act the way you do because you want to change the memory of the hurt you experienced as a child.**

   a. Simon wishes life was not so hard. It seems all the bad luck comes his way when others get good breaks in life. He wants life to treat him equally, but he feels the scale is tipped against him. He does not want to believe life will be hard; he wants to believe he can make business ventures successful for himself.

   b. His thoughts and actions are always focused on the belief that he will not be successful. He anticipates failure and expects things to go wrong. He *always* notices his failures and *never* notices all the things that go right. These thoughts and actions are aligned with his belief that things will always go wrong for him.

c. Simon sees that he keeps trying to find new business ideas that will get him out of the rut because he wants to change the pain in his life. He wants to prove wrong the lie that he will never be a success. But his belief about himself causes all his actions to sabotage his efforts. Despite his attempts, he believes they won't be successful, so they never are.

d. He sees that every previous attempt was based on an attempt to change the hurt from his childhood. He realizes that nothing today can change the childhood hurt.

5. **Choose a new belief.**

a. Simon now recognizes that his old belief is a false belief he developed as a child, and that he has control to set new beliefs. He has chosen to believe that things won't go wrong and that life is not against him. Since he no longer holds onto the hurt from his childhood, he does not need financial success to be happy. This allows him to pursue success for fun without fear of failing.

6. **Change your actions and thoughts to align with your new belief.**

a. Simon has learned to see all the positive things in his life and now notices them more than the negative things. He is optimistic about what good things can happen instead of worrying about and anticipating what bad things might happen.

7. **Choose to forgive and choose to love.**

    a. Simon forgives his parents for telling him that he will have such a hard time in life. He forgives God for allowing a life of struggle, and he forgives himself for believing a lie about himself for such a long time.

Where is my Source?
The location is hidden,
but waits to be found.

Could it be in me?
The secret beneath the layers;
the Source inside me.

CHAPTER 3

Look Inside Yourself

This chapter shows where to look to find the secret. This is *Step Three* of the **Ten Steps to Finding the Secret Inside**. When you learn how to look in the right place, you will be able to find what no one can tell you. This book points in the direction to look, and suggests things to look for. The answers found will be unique to bring you peace, happiness, and good fortune in a way nothing and no one else can bring.

Ten Steps to Finding the Secret Inside

1. Understand your current perception
2. Heal your emotional pain
3. *Look inside yourself*
4. Choose new beliefs
5. Live in the present
6. Find creative power within you

7. Be emotionally aware
8. Align your personality
9. Embrace what "Is"
10. Transcend the illusion

The secret of what is missing from your life is hidden inside you. In order to access it you must learn to turn off your mind and meditate. This is the way to connect with the miracle. You've probably heard people refer to words and phrases such as:

Sixth sense
Inner peace
The God inside
Spiritual dimension
Out-of-body experience
Transcendental meditation
States of consciousness
Quiet your mind
Turn off your mind
Spiritual awareness
Between thoughts
Being present

All these words and phrases are simply attempts to explain people's meditation experiences. You can choose whatever words you want to describe yours. If the idea of meditation appears overwhelming or confusing, you do not understand what it is. It is the most natural and easy thing you will ever do, yet it can change your life forever if you want it to and if you allow it. Unless you believe in the benefits of meditation, it will have no meaning to you. You have the choice to believe or not. If you choose to believe you will be changed in a positive way forever.

You have heard the saying "you can give a man a fish and he will eat for a day, or you can teach a man to fish and he will eat for a lifetime." It is most important that you learn how to find the answers for yourself rather than be told the answers. Your answers may be different than mine. Below I've defined four things to do in order to find the secrets. If you do this while believing, you will learn how to fish for the miracle inside you.

Four Steps to Finding the Miracle Inside You
1. Have Faith — Believe Without Seeing
2. Set Aside Preconceived Beliefs
3. Meditate to Connect With Your Inner Self
4. Trust Your Sixth Sense

1. Have Faith — Believe Without Seeing

This is a common theme in many religions, but it is not very often applied to finding the miracle inside you. Religions use this idea to get you to trust that what you are told is the truth. Here you learn how to fish for your own truth. First, you need to believe that there is a truth to be found and that there is a place inside you to find it.

Most people think like this:

+ Show me, then I will believe.
+ I see myself; therefore, I believe I am this way.
+ I see the world; therefore, I believe it is that way.

To find the secret of the miracle, start believing the opposite, like this:

✦ Believe first, then it will be shown to me.
✦ Believe that the answers are inside, then, I will find the answers.

If you have any reservation or doubt about wasting any more time with this idea, consider your choices:

a. If there are no secrets of a miracle inside, they won't appear, no matter how hard you want them to be there. So go ahead and give it a try. If you find nothing, at least you tried.

b. If there are secrets of a miracle inside, but you never look for them, you will miss out on a lifetime of happiness, prosperity, and peace.

c. If secrets of a miracle do exist inside you, and you go in to look for them, you will find them and your life will be positively changed forever.

If you have not found the connection to the Source inside you, then you instinctively know your life is still missing something.

No matter what you believe about how the universe came into existence and how you came into existence, have faith to believe there is a clue inside you to show the answer. You do not need any religion to tell you what is right or wrong; the Source inside will show you.

You won't be able to experience this process unless you go into it believing it is there to be found. The first step is to believe that inside you is your path to the "Source."

By believing this Source exists, you allow it to step out of the shadows and show itself to you. Without belief, it will not show itself to you.

2.   Set Aside Preconceived Beliefs

All your beliefs came into being because of the way you saw yourself and the world around you. Remember you saw things first and later came to believe them to be that way. You see things in a biased way based on your own preferences and previous experiences; you may not see them the way they really are. Therefore your beliefs may not reflect the truth.

Set aside all those beliefs and assume every one of them is wrong. If you want to find the truth about yourself and about everything else, do not assume anything you previously thought to be true. If you want the Source inside you to show you truth, you must be open to accept whatever you find.

Forget that you have any beliefs and opinions. Be as a child recently born who has no idea about anything and who is exploring their own nature to find clues about who they are and where they came from.

If you search with an open mind, you will find what is there. If you search with preconceived ideas, you will find things that look exactly as you already believe them to be. And your life will go on exactly as it is now. You must believe there are new answers for you to find in order for them to become visible to you.

3.   Meditate to Connect With Your Inner Self

One form of meditation is being quiet in your mind, not

thinking, but listening to the quietness when you stop thinking. Some people call this place "your inner self." If you do not yet believe that you have an inner self, then this is a good time to practice believing without yet seeing. All you need to do is learn how to make your mind quiet by making it stop thinking.

This is the practice called "experiencing your inner self," but it is not important what name you give it as long as you believe it is there. When you believe it exists and learn to be quiet in your mind, you will be shown what you want to know.

You might be used to letting your mind run loose. Realize that it takes a little while to get it to slow down and stop thinking on its own. Do not be discouraged when it feels awkward at first. You might have never experienced turning off your mind, but you will soon learn to do it through practice. Prayer is a word to describe talking to God. Meditation is the opposite; it is learning to stop talking and be quiet so the Source can speak to you.

Practice meditation when you are not tired. Find a quiet place where you can sit or lie without thinking about anything. Do nothing but breathe. When your mind starts to think, notice it and stop it. Thoughts may return; notice and keep stopping them. Your mind is undisciplined and might never have had to be obedient to you. It might take some practice to get it under control.

When meditating, it may help to imagine yourself as a cat waiting to pounce on a mouse. But you are waiting without thought … waiting … waiting … waiting to ensure your mind does not start thinking. And when it does start thinking, stop it and go back to not thinking.

By practicing this exercise you will be able to wait for a few seconds or more each time without a thought. This exercise teaches that you are separate from your mind. For brief moments you will experience your inner self waiting for your mind to think.

Your inner self exists and your mind exists, and they are two separate parts of you. Learning to quiet your mind is the foundation for other types of meditation — for relaxing, for setting your future into motion, and for hearing the Source tell you the things you want to know.

Practicing this form of meditation enables you to go longer periods of time in a relaxed state without letting your mind control you. When you get control of your mind you will be able to turn it on and off as you desire. This is the foundation needed to be able to connect with your Source inside you; or in other words to find the secret of the miracle inside.

> *The miracle is that you have within yourself a connection to your Source. When you quiet your mind you become connected with it. With practice you learn to experience many miracles in this state of being connected with your Source. It is in this state where you learn to create your future and receive guidance for your life. You come to realize that you are not just connecting with the Source of everything, but you are in fact a part of it. You are connected to everything in every way.*

This place in the quiet of your mind is your true self as opposed to who you always thought you were. With practice you will find that this form of meditation is both peaceful and relaxing. It gives you access to see yourself as a part of the divine energy and consciousness of the universe. The more time you spend in this relaxed state, the more you associate yourself with this inner part of you rather than with your personality.

When you meditate you are teaching yourself a couple of important things. You are showing that there is another part of yourself that is completely separate from your body and mind. The more you learn to turn off your mind, the more you will convince yourself that your mind is separate from this other part of you.

Putting yourself in this state connects you to your Source. While in this state you may or may not hear the Source or what it might want to tell you. That is normal; you are still practicing the state of being connected to Source.

When you are convinced that you have an inner self separate from your thinking mind, it is time to experience a higher level of consciousness by communicating with the Source. While meditating, ask the Source to show you whatever it is you want to know. You might want to know how to be happy, how to find who you really are, how to find love, or how to heal from emotional pain.

After you ask, *know* that the Source will bring you the answer. But do not expect the answer to come right away. The act of meditating sets into motion the spiritual energy to request information from the Source. It may not answer you immediately and it may answer you in a number of different ways that you do not expect. Just ask the question and go into the state of quieting your mind and strengthening the connection between you and your inner self so that you will be in a state of mind to recognize an answer when it is shown to you.

There are many ways that the Source provides answers and guidance to you. It is possible that while meditating with a quiet mind you receive insight. You can usually tell the difference between receiving insight from your Source and hearing your own mind thinking. Your mind thinks about things that you expect — work, problems, family issues, tasks you need to accomplish, worries, and concerns. When you receive insight from your Source during meditation it is usually something totally unrelated to what you would normally think about. It seems to come "out of the blue."

When this occurs, practice having faith and believing without seeing. Believe that the Source has shown you an answer to your question, even if it does not make any sense at the moment. Insights from the Source, like dreams, are always very subtle. When you are new to sensing them, you feel as if you are making them up in your own mind. Ask yourself if this is a thought you would have initiated or if it seems more like a thought that popped into your head out of nowhere. If it popped out of nowhere, then it was given to you by the Source inside you. Take it and believe it was given to you by the Source. Hold onto it and think what it could mean; maybe days or weeks later it will all become clear to you.

If you want to become more confident in how this works, practice every day. Within a few fifteen-minute sessions you should be able to turn off your mind each time you try, even if only for fifteen seconds at a time. Your mind might keep trying to think as often as you turn it off, but that is all right; you are learning. Soon your mind will cooperate more with your desire to quiet it. Within a few weeks of practice you should be able to request guidance for many areas of your life and you should sense a very relaxed state of meditation when you do this.

There is nothing tense or forced about meditation. You do not need to be in a yoga position or any other special position. It should be the most natural thing you ever do. It is simply relaxing without a care or worry in the world and asking for input from the inner part of you which is directly connected to the infinite universe of spirit.

If you practice this form of meditation and have asked for guidance then be prepared to *sense* the answer in a number of ways.

4.   Trust Your Sixth Sense

You might have heard about a term called your "sixth sense." Physically, your body has five ways to sense input from your world: sight, smell, touch, hearing, and taste. Any other way you sense something is what is sometimes called the sixth sense. It usually refers to sensing things on a spiritual level or in the invisible realm. Have faith and believe you have this sixth sense which allows you to sense the guiding force in your life in many ways. It is your own inner self being connected to the infinite intelligence and consciousness of the universe which I call your Source.

Terms related to the sixth sense are:

Dreams	Gut feelings
Visions	Conscious
Déjà vu	Intuition
Hunch	Voice inside you

Practice believing-without-yet-seeing by believing there are signs all around you every day to show you something through your sixth sense. After meditating and seeking information from the Source, believe that you will find answers through many signs that will be shown to you.

You might get a *feeling* about something, or have a dream, or sense a voice inside, or you might see a vision during meditation. All of these are ways that the Source gives you clues and gives you answers. You might not understand them at first. In time you will learn more about what is happening to you and what it means. When you see these signs, you are seeing the world as it really exists in a multi-dimensional state, both physical and spiritual.

You have a choice to either ignore your sixth sense or to embrace it. This connection to the Source of everything in the universe exists whether you embrace it or not. Ignoring it only keeps you living without the input and guidance of infinite wisdom. Pay attention to your sixth sense and learn to understand it. You will gain insight into who you are and how to find complete happiness, freedom, and prosperity forever.

Each time you have a dream, ask yourself what it means. Ask what is happening and to whom is it happening. Believe that nothing happens by accident; every dream is an opportunity for you to become connected with the infinite intelligence of the universe. You are a part of it. It is showing you the reality of the entire universe of which you are a part. If you don't know what a dream means, then ask the Source for help while meditating.

When you dream of someone you know, pick up the phone and say you felt inspired to call. It may be as simple as that — you were supposed to call them. The messages do not need to be earth-shaking.

When you experience déjà vu, ask yourself why it feels as though you have been here and experienced this before. This is likely a message for you. Do not ignore it just because you cannot understand it. If you are unsure, ask the Source to tell you. Then meditate with a quiet mind and see what comes to you.

While meditating, you might "see things" in your mind. It might be your mind day-dreaming about your life and you will need to notice and stop your mind. You will recognize the thoughts as things your mind normally thinks about. This will probably happen a lot at first, but don't get discouraged. Keep stopping the thoughts and go back to a quiet mind.

Many forms of meditation speak about the importance of your breathing during meditation. This is simply because breathing can be a tool to quiet the mind. When your mind starts thinking, bring it back to concentrate on your breathing. Breathe in … breathe out … breathe in … breathe out. This takes a small amount of thinking, but it is a transition step between a wild uncontrolled mind and one that can become calm and quiet just before entering a stage of complete and deep meditation, devoid of thought.

When you have attained "thoughtlessness," you might see flashes of light, colors, stars, or a picture. This is spontaneous. You will know when you see visions because they are unrelated to what your mind normally thinks about.

When these occur, note what you see. Be still and let it unfold before you. Don't think about what should happen, just keep your mind turned off and observe what is being shown to you. A vision might only be about colors or light and shapes, and you may wonder what meaning it has. The meaning is in the emotions that you feel related to what you see. Ask yourself what you feel during this experience. Even if you don't get an answer right away, the experience strengthens your belief that there is an inner part of you connected to the infinite universe that shows you things. If you want to know more about the meaning of some things, keep asking and searching for clues.

Some visions look like a movie unfolding before your eyes

while your eyes are closed in meditation. If this is a day dream, stop and turn off your mind. But, if it is a spontaneous scene out of *nowhere*, watch it and observe. These visions might last for about a minute or less. Trust that this is a message for you, but do not be discouraged if the message is not yet clear.

Once you have begun the process of reconnecting with your Source, you will notice that you have the ability to sense things, even when you are not in a state of meditation. While engaged in normal activity you may suddenly get a feeling that someone is watching you, but you find no one around. Trust that the Source is making itself known to your conscious mind. Take such an opportunity to believe without seeing. Believe that the Source is trying to get your attention. Speak to it and say that you are aware of it and you are listening. Ask what it is trying to tell you. Is there something you should be doing or someone you should call? The message does not need to be related to the original feeling that got your attention.

Next time you get a *gut feeling* or *"intuition,"* don't ignore it. If it tells you to do something, respond and tell it you trust it to guide you. Respond in whatever way you feel it is guiding you. You may not always get confirmation that this is right, but many times you will. Even when you are unsure, trust that the Source is leading you.

Other times you might be working on a project when something goes wrong. Occasionally there are interruptions, three or four in a row. When that happens, recognize that this is probably the Source trying to get your attention. Ask why this is happening. Maybe you are supposed to put aside what you are working on for a while; ask why.

The more you become connected to the Source the more you will pay attention whenever something out of the ordinary happens to you. Eventually, it can become *ordinary* for you to operate in a state of connection with the Source, being led and guided on a regular basis. This takes a great deal of discipline as well as surrender to achieve this level. *I am still working to attain it.*

However you sense the Source, believe that it wants to show you something. If your car battery dies and you find yourself stranded, don't get annoyed at the inconvenience, but recognize that the Source went to great lengths to get your attention. It may be that you are supposed to meet someone who stops to assist you. It might be that you are supposed to be late to your appointment. Since this event may alter the course of activities in your day, trust that this change is intended to happen for a good reason. It is your responsibility to look for what it might be. You will often find the answers as long as you look for them.

All of these things require believing without seeing. You believe first. By doing so, you open the door to the opportunity of seeing what it all means. But without the belief that all things in your life have an intended meaning you will never be able to see the purpose of life's so-called problems.

Life is full of messages every day. The Source will show you which way to turn on a road when you are lost: it will prompt you to speak to a stranger that you are supposed to meet; it will prompt you to call a friend who needs to hear from you. It will point you to any number of normal and seemingly insignificant things. These are the things that change people's lives; they alter the course of the future in a way to make it divinely good in every way. Your Source can guide you to a new job, a new relationship, a family, a career, financial success, a new location, freedom, peace and happiness. You are free to ask for whatever you desire, just be sure to look for and accept the many ways that the answers will be shown to you.

Those who start practicing meditation are like new-born babies. A baby may not understand every word spoken to it, but it knows the emotions and it senses the spirit of those around it. At first you will not know what many things mean; it may not seem like you are getting intelligent messages from anything. Be patient and don't give up. There is no hurry; you have a lifetime to figure it out.

The important thing is that you believe in the connection between you and the infinite universe, the Source. With practice you will come to know many new things. Eventually you will hear clear direction. You will become used to hearing wisdom telling you helpful things. You will become empowered to create things in your life with just thoughts. You will learn to use the power of creation to build a wonderful life that you never imagined possible.

This is the secret that you are looking for, the secret so many people never know. Most people look outside themselves for everything when, in fact, the answer to everything is the connection inside to the infinite Source. You are connected to infinite intelligence that knows everything about the past and everything about the future. You are connected to everything in the universe because everything is connected to this same infinite intelligence.

The secret is how to access it. Now you know that you need to look inside yourself, and you know how to do it. Turn off your mind and listen. The miracle is the connection between your inner self and the infinite Source. In essence you are part of the Source, but it is hidden by the busy-ness of your own mind.

When you were young
you saw things first,
then you believed.

Now you are older,
if you believe first;
then you will see.

CHAPTER 4

Choose New Beliefs

This chapter shows how to develop new beliefs which will bring about the results you want for your life. You will learn why you need to replace old beliefs with new ones and how to do that. You will find examples of fundamental beliefs that have existed for millennia and which continue to be re-discovered by those who search for guidance within themselves. This is **Step Four** of the **Ten Steps to Finding the Secret Inside**.

Ten Steps to Finding the Secret Inside

1. Understand your current perception
2. Heal your emotional pain
3. Look inside yourself
4. *Choose new beliefs*
5. Live in the present
6. Find creative power within you

7.   Be emotionally aware
8.   Align your personality
9.   Embrace what "Is"
10. Transcend the illusion

Why New Beliefs Are Necessary

New beliefs are necessary if your current beliefs are producing anything less that a life filled with happiness and peace and good feelings. Your beliefs determine the quality of your life and the way everything looks and feels to you. If there is any part of your life or the world around you that does not feel perfect and good, you can change it by changing your beliefs.

Your fundamental beliefs were likely formed when you were a small child and they may never have changed. They were formed with limited knowledge and life experiences. They were based on a limited view of yourself and were influenced by the culture around you and by the traditions you were taught.

Fundamental beliefs do not mean your political beliefs or similar beliefs that change with time as you mature and become more educated. Fundamental beliefs are those that define who you think you are; your value, your esteem, your capabilities, and your origin.

As a child you did not know that the way things appear is a direct result of the way you believe them to be. If you start with a pre-conceived idea about the way something is supposed to be, then the world will manifest itself to be seen that way. Because of this, your beliefs influenced the way you saw yourself and the world. You accepted the way it looked and believed it to exist as you perceived it. This caused you to accept things about yourself and the world around you that probably were not true.

The culture in which you grew up influenced your view of the way things appear. Consider that if you were born into Western society, you likely believe in a God, one that is not here right now, but rather "up in heaven."

If you grew up in an Eastern culture, you will have been influenced by a belief that the divine Source of all things is unlimited, that it does not reside anywhere specifically but rather in all places, in all things, at all times. Eastern thought believes the Source cannot be in one form or another, nor in one place or another. Most significantly, the divine Source resides in everything, including you and me. Additionally we are part of it.

Truth should not be dependent upon the part of the world in which you were born. Truth and beliefs should be based on the way things really are. When you were a child, you did not know you were being influenced by your culture. You simply believed what you saw. You did not know you were being influenced by the traditions or religions you were taught. You simply accepted what *appeared* to be true.

Look at your beliefs today. New beliefs may be necessary because the ones you have might not be true. They might bring dissatisfaction and they might limit you from having a satisfied, happy, and wonderful life. You may feel nothing is wrong with your beliefs. However, if your life is anything less than perfect love and peace, you need to consider changing some of your fundamental beliefs. Every belief you have influences how you feel; every belief is worth examining and rebuilding or replacing.

How to Form New Beliefs

Truth cannot be proved or disproved, but it can be tested by the divine Source inside you. Truth is written inside you, and it knows what is right for your life. Truth for someone else may not be truth for your life. When you seek your inner self and connect with the Source, you will find your truth.

A lot of people want to tell you to believe what they believe. What is right for them may or may not be right for you because you are not living the same life experience as they are. Your destiny might be different from theirs. No religion can prove it has the right answer for you. Each religion is one person's attempt to explain God in terms that were revealed to them alone. Seek your own inspiration, not the ones given to someone else.

When establishing new beliefs, don't allow yourself to be influenced by the following things:

A. Culture — Do not accept beliefs just because they are the trend or common belief of your culture. There is no depth here or personal guidance for your individual life.
B. Appearance — Do not accept beliefs that just appear to be true. Everything may look distorted because of your preconceived ideas.
C. Teachings — Do not blindly accept beliefs from people who have taught you in the past, or from religious doctrines. These are someone else's personal experiences that became truth for them. Rather, seek your own personal experience to become inspired.

The three items listed above probably influenced most of the beliefs you currently hold. Examine the results of them in your life. Are you blissfully happy and feeling good all the time? Does the world appear all good to you? If not, then consider using better foundations on which to base new beliefs.

Cultural beliefs likely promote the idea of a God separate from you. This translates to all creation being separate and not connected to God or to its other parts. This allows for conflict, disagreement, and wars throughout the world. By following what culture tells you to believe, you are not making your own choices about your beliefs.

The beliefs you formed as a result of the appearance of things have caused pain in your life. You probably already see how some of the things you came to believe about yourself as a child caused life-long pain. Yet now you see they do not need to be true. You believed a lie because it *appeared* to be that way and you accepted it.

Teachings between the East and West are so opposite in fundamentals that there is little to debate. Western religions, however, have similar fundamentals to each other that raise debate over the numerous details of doctrine. See how useless it is to adopt one of these teachings? They are different people's ideas of what truth is. The Christian Bible contains writing by different people about their inspirations. None of these are your inspirations from your Source. Other people, hundreds of years later, translated the Bible according to *their* inspirations, not yours. And teachers today teach it according to *their* inspirations, not yours.

Determine to move away from your past method of forming beliefs. Use the following criteria to guide that process:

A. Your Life — Determine to believe in things that are aligned with what you want.

B. Peace — Determine to believe in things that bring peace to you.

C. Inspiration — Seek personal inspiration to determine your beliefs.

Define What You Want to Believe for Your Life

You've already experienced a lifetime of being influenced by what you *should* believe; now take the opportunity to define what you *want* to believe. The things you observed as a child caused you to form beliefs that now you don't want to be true. Let those experiences direct you toward what you do want to believe.

Earlier, you were asked to search your memory to find the experiences of your childhood that brought about painful emotions. You found beliefs that you assumed to be true about yourself. These are some of the beliefs that you no longer want to be true. State the opposite of these beliefs as examples of what you might wish were true.

For example:

✦ You might have developed a belief that you were not loved by a parent, and you wish it were not true. Now, choose to define a new belief that you are loved by your parents, by God, by friends, and by everyone in the whole world. Don't rationalize as yet whether or not you feel this is true; that step will come later. Right now you are creating a list of beliefs that you *wish* to be true.

✦ You might have developed a belief that you could never be as successful as other people and you wish it were not that way.

Define a new belief that you are capable of achieving anything you desire.

+ You might have developed a belief that you were not valuable and you wish it were not true. Define a new belief that you are infinitely valuable, more than any material objects. You are equal to all other people in the universe *and* equal to God because you are a part of the Source of everything. The Source is in you!

+ You might have grown up feeling dependent upon others to lead you, and you wish you were more independent. Define a new belief that you are capable of directing your life in the exact details you want.

+ You might have learned that you cannot trust anyone to protect you or love you, and you wish this were not true. Define a new belief that you can trust the universe to do everything to plan for perfection in your life. Trust that everything is on purpose and exactly as planned; there are no such things as accidents.

Consider the following and choose the belief you want to be true for you.

+ Decide whether you prefer to believe in a God that created you out of nothing, or if you prefer to believe *you are part of* the consciousness that made you and everything else.

+ Decide whether you prefer to believe you are dependent upon a God that is outside of yourself, or if you prefer to believe *you are* an acting living part of the Source of everything.

✦ Decide whether you prefer to believe your life is predestined to be a certain way or if you prefer to believe *you have the power to direct your life.*

✦ Decide whether you prefer to believe your life was created out of nothing and is primarily physical in nature, or if you prefer to believe you have always been a living spirit which has existed from before the beginning of time and which will last for eternity.

✦ Decide whether you prefer to believe you are separate from the spirit of God, separate from other people, and separate from nature, or if you prefer to believe all things are connected and all things are a part of each other.

✦ Decide whether you prefer to believe that accidents and coincidences happen, or if you prefer to believe that there are no accidents and no coincidences because all things are connected and part of a divine plan.

✦ Decide whether you prefer to believe that evil happens, people get hurt, life is not fair, people suffer, tragedies exist, or if you prefer to believe everything is *good*. (Even what appears as tragic is only because you cannot see or understand the perfect plan occurring before you.)

Using all the suggested decisions above, make your own list of the things you wish were true, the things you want to believe.

Define the Results You Want to Bring You Peace

Beliefs influence the results you get by the way you *see* yourself and the world around you. They also influence the way you *feel* about yourself and the way you feel about the world around you. After you have made a list of the beliefs you wish were true, make a list of the results you want in your life. Use the experiences that you don't like in your life to guide you to define the experiences that you do want in your life.

For example: make a list similar to the one below, but based on your own specific details:

How I Don't Like to Feel	How I Want to Feel
Unloved	Loved
Poor	Rich
Frustrated with my situation	Happy
Worried and fearful	Peaceful
Controlled by other people	In control of my life
I don't get what I want	I always get what I want
Life is unfair to me	Everything is fair
Not trusting of people	Trust for others
Everything goes wrong	Everything happens perfectly
God didn't answer me	I hear and see Source everywhere

Seek to Be Inspired

Seeking inspiration is by far the most natural, fun, and yet mysterious part of the process of choosing new beliefs. It is natural because you were made to do this; it is mysterious because you might never have known you were made to do this and you might not know how.

Review what you have done so far in the process of choosing new beliefs:

✦ You've agreed to ignore influences from cultural preferences, past teachings, or the way things appear to be.

✦ You've agreed to choose beliefs based on what you want, what brings peace, and what you get inspired to believe.

✦ You've compiled a list of things you want to believe.

✦ You've made a list of results you want in your life.

By doing what is listed above you have set into motion a search to find beliefs that match your desires. You have sent out energy to the universe to reconcile the conflicts between your old beliefs and the new ones. Use meditation to let your inner self connect with the Source and to be led to the truth for your life.

In preparing to meditate, review the beliefs you wish to be true for your life along with the results you want for your life. Go into meditation and ask the Source to show you truth as it relates to your beliefs. Ask the Source to show you whether your old beliefs or your new proposed beliefs are truth. Practice making your mind quiet, and stop it when it attempts to think. Be still and listen.

You will be shown things either while meditating or later; do not be discouraged if you find nothing during the meditation itself. The important thing is to connect with that state of being quiet in your mind. At those moments between thoughts, you are living and operating in a state of being one with your Source. That is all it takes to connect and start the process.

This process allows the Source to hear your request and initiate action to bring answers to your conscious mind. The answers may come in meditation, by a feeling, a voice, or a picture. Even as it occurs, you may or may not understand the meaning, but the more you practice this technique the more you will learn about it. What is shown to you has meaning only for you, while what is shown to another has meaning only for them.

If you do not sense any answer during meditation, believe you are doing the right thing anyway. Trust your sixth sense to find the answer later. Even when you are not meditating, make a conscious effort to be open to sensing answers to your requests. The answers may vary. You may watch a television show or a movie that inspires you in a way that you feel is an answer to your request. A movie may have a theme that strengthens the belief you want to have; when you notice it, you sense the connection. When you sense it, trust that this is an answer for you.

You might meet someone who says something that relates to one of the beliefs you want to have. Trust it is an answer to your request. The signs come to you when you believe they will. The results act like signposts pointing toward a direction to believe.

You might have a dream that relates to something you want to believe. Trust it was not a random dream. Many other situations will come to you over the following days and weeks which relate to what you seek answers for.

Realize that you have spent a lifetime reinforcing the beliefs you initiated as a child; it may take some time to redirect them into new beliefs. Depending on where you are in the process, you may go fast or slow in changing your beliefs. Either way, you will see answers to what you seek as long as you believe you will see them.

As you notice signs and answers, continue to use meditation daily to connect with the Source and to ask for guidance to help you form your new beliefs.

When you sense inspiration about one or more of these new beliefs, grab onto it and plant it firmly into your life. Do this by using another form of meditation: program your mind to believe what you tell it to believe. Choose the new belief you want and state it to your inner self. Then imagine it working in your life.

If you want to believe that you can be happy and peaceful despite what happens to you, then imagine it. Don't let your mind wander and day dream, but do cause it to think during this part of the meditation. You have now gained control of your mind to turn it on and off as you desire. This time you want it turned on and controlled by you. Imagine yourself being happy and peaceful. Imagine what that means in as much detail as you can create.

It might mean you are full of energy, smiling, and able to do the things you want to do at a slow pace without having to hurry through the day. See yourself doing all the things you like and want to be doing. See yourself able to leave your job if it is not what you love to do. See yourself doing what you love to do. See yourself in the country or state where you love to be. See yourself healthy. See yourself with as much money as you want. See yourself connected to your Source every moment.

Visualization is a form of meditation. It trains the mind to believe in what you want to occur and at the same time sets into motion the energy to create exactly what you imagine for your life. Believe that no matter what happens, you will continue to trust that the Source is in control and that nothing else matters as much as keeping your peace and happiness. As you do this form of meditation regularly, you will become convinced that this is true.

Use these meditation practices to seek guidance. When you hear an answer, use meditation to plant the beliefs firmly into your life. Then test the beliefs by determining how they make you feel.

You made a list of the results you want in your life. Some of those results might include happiness, health, wealth, finding a partner, or other things. Now that you are meditating and planting the beliefs in your mind, test them against the results.

Ask yourself how you feel about your life compared to how you felt before you started this process. Are you experiencing more or less peace, more or less happiness, more or less of all the other results you wanted to see? If you have chosen the correct beliefs for your life and received inspiration from your Source, then everything should be getting better. This is your feedback system. If you feel worse about anything, examine that belief and go back through the process. Most of the time the beliefs you chose are correct for you and that is why you wanted them in the first place.

Occasionally, there remains a bad feeling that needs to be fixed. Even after going through the process, you might experience fear or some other negative emotion. If this happens, ask yourself what belief is causing this. Ask if that might have been an inappropriate belief, since it is causing a problem. Repeat the process to form a new and better belief that allows you to see the results you want.

Some Foundational Beliefs That Have Existed for Millennia

You must form the beliefs that work for you. No one else can do this for you. In order to understand the range of ideas available to you, it is good to learn what others before you have found. This does not mean you should believe the same way others do unless the Source inside you shows you it is the way for you.

Over the course of thousands of years people have searched for meaning to the universe and their place within it. You are not the first to search for something missing in life. It seems reasonable to assume that others have also come across answers that helped them with this common search.

> I wish to share two foundational beliefs that are, to me, of great value related to this topic. These are beliefs you can give thought to, then ask the Source within to reveal if they are truths for you. I share these ideas in my own way, but the ideas are ones that have been discovered by people searching inside themselves for thousands of years.

First Common Belief — A Divine Source

A common theme that resonates with people across the world and which spans thousands of years is the concept of a divine Source responsible for the creation of everything in existence. The Source has consciousness to know and understand all things; it is intelligent. Western religions call this entity God, although those who seek within themselves rarely use that word to describe it. The Source is much more than words can adequately describe.

This Source is the collective consciousness of all other beings — you and me and all other living things. It does not need to reside in any one particular place because it resides in all the places it has created. Since it is in all places at all times it does not make sense to call it a "being with a form." It is more appropriate to think of it as infinite energy with intelligence and purpose.

In order to understand how this Source relates to you and me, consider the following analogy. Imagine before the beginning of time and before anything is created that the Source existed in one spot. Imagine it is shaped as a sphere floating in space. It contains within it time and space and everything that exists.

This sphere is the Source of all things; all things start here and exist here and end here. Nothing exists outside the sphere. This is the Source of everything. Within this sphere nothing is separate; it is one homogeneous entity.

There is no separation of physical and spiritual, actions and emotions, love and hatred, happiness and sadness. They are all part of the Source. There is no separation between humans, plants, and animals. In this way all things exist. There is no recognition of what is contained within the sphere because there is no contrast between all the things it contains.

The Source is intelligent and has the ability to think and reason. It has the ability to learn and improve infinitely. In order to do that it chooses to separate itself into many different forms of energy and matter and emotions and ideas in order to gain new experience within itself.

Creation Was Birthed

As a way for the Source to experience new things, it separated into an infinite number of parts in order for them to interact with each other. The Source which existed in one place became many parts in many places, all separated to look like individual parts. Even though all the parts appeared separate, they are linked together because they are still part of the Source.

Many things became separate in order to be seen as individual parts — things such as time and space, light and dark, good and bad, spiritual and physical, seen and unseen, matter, and energy. The universe and planets and life and nature were formed from this matter. You and I are one part of this Source. We appear as individuals, yet we are a part of the whole at all times.

Another analogy of the divine Source is one of a pitcher full of water. The pitcher contains a million drops of water. If a thousand droplets are sprinkled on the ground, each drop appears as a separate drop. If the drops could speak, they would say that they are isolated drops of water. They each roll on the ground and take on their own appearances because some drops get muddy while others get polluted with other forms of debris and grime.

If the drops could speak, they would say something like "The water in the pitcher is my Source, but I am not like it because I am only a dirty drop." The drops would view water in the pitcher as their creator. But they would not consider themselves anything like the pitcher of water because they are much smaller and dirtier.

Eventually, at the right time, a droplet will awaken to realize who it is and where it came from. When this occurs it realizes that it is not the mud; it is the pure water underneath the mud. It recognizes that it is the same as the water in the pitcher. It sees how it came out of the pitcher and is identical to the water in the pitcher except for the mud it picked up along the way. In fact, it is the same water as the water in the pitcher. There is no difference; it came out of the pitcher and can be cleaned and put back in. When it is reunited, there is no separation.

The same is true with you and your Source. You came out and picked up layers of personality, but underneath it all you are still the spirit of the Source from where you came. You appear separated from all the other parts, but remember, the appearance of things is only an illusion. You are one with the Source.

You are made identical to the Source, and I am made identical to the Source. You and I and everyone are therefore the same;

the very exact same thing. You are masked from seeing it by the illusion of the body, mind, and personality you think you are. As you awaken, you become more like me, and I more like you, until we become one with our Source and one with each other.

Emotions of anger, hate, sorrow, love, happiness, and all the rest are a part of the creation. Actions of love, birthing, planting, sowing, reaping, stealing, and working, are a part of creation. One part of the Source may choose to live the life of a priest; another part may choose to live the life of a thief. Some parts of the Source choose to be horses; some become plants, some rocks, and some the wind. No part of the Source is "good" or "bad." All are parts of the whole.

Love cannot be perceived until it is separated from hatred and fear. Hate provides a contrast to see what love is, and love provides the contrast to see what hate is. All things must be separated in order to experience their individual aspects. The purpose for creation is to better understand the individual components contained within the Source. These parts interact with one another in order for the whole Source to learn and improve. It displays millions of parts; some we label "good" and some we label "bad." In reality none are good and none are bad; they are all parts of the whole.

When you learn to see this, you can stop making judgments about what is good or bad. You will know they are all part of the Source displayed in different ways. People and their actions are never evil or bad; they are all part of the Source.

Many of the things people do bring themselves pain because they don't see themselves as part of the Source. They see themselves as separate people who must protect themselves from pain. The Source that created everything cannot feel pain or sorrow. When you feel pain, the purpose of that pain is to cause you to look within yourself for a better solution to life, to find your true self.

The reason for life is to experience the fullness of the Source, and therefore the fullness of you. In order to get the entire benefit of the human experience, you allowed yourself to forget who you were when you were born. If you were conscious of the divinity in you, you would not have allowed yourself to feel pain and suffering. But in order to gain the experience you desired, you allowed yourself to be born into an illusion of seeing yourself as separate from the Source, temporarily.

You can choose at any time to remember your divinity and reunite to become one with Source. Now that you are awakening, you can choose to get out of the illusion, because being in the illusion feels bad. Before you were born you planned for yourself to eventually discover your own divinity by remembering who you are. You planted that idea inside you so that one day you could discover it when the time was right. That time has come; otherwise you would not be reading this book now.

When you remember that you are not separate, but rather a part of the Source, you will again see the beauty of everything. You will use your power to create love, joy, good health, happiness, and goodness in the world all around you. You only need to remember how to do it.

Remembering Your Divinity

Because you are an extension of the Source, your purpose is to experience things in order to learn and grow. You do this by first remembering that you are part of the Source and by remembering you have all the abilities it has. Since you have existed forever as a part of the Source, you already know everything; you just need to remember it. You do this by connecting with it through meditation.

Creating an illusion that you are separate from the Source allows you to experience feeling hurt without really getting hurt, as in a dream. If you wish to end the experience of pain and struggle, you can make the divine decision to end the pain now. Return to the deity that you have always been a part of; return to the connection with your Source. You may have to overcome a lifetime of programming, and it may take time, but it can be done.

Second Common Belief — Life is Intentional

When Source separated itself into parts to create the universe, it set into motion everything to happen in the exact way to bring about the perfect and intended result. The first common belief is that such a Source exists and is responsible for creating all that exists, and that you are a part of that Source. The second common belief is that all events happening within creation are part of an intentional plan.

When you awaken to know who you are, you see the world as the perfect place that it is and you see love all around. The universe and all things happening in it are orchestrated to bring about love and beauty in the world. If you see the world in any other way than perfect and full of love, your perspective is inaccurate.

If you look at the world and cannot see love everywhere, consider changing your perspective by changing your beliefs. Make new beliefs that allow you to see the world as a place full of love and beauty. The Bible says that after creation God spoke and said it is all good. Choose to believe *all* things are intentional and on purpose.

If you want to change your life to be one filled with only love, happiness and goodness, all you need to do is choose beliefs that make that possible. Choose to believe that all your life occurrences are intentional and for a good purpose.

When you believe this, you can find the good in all situations. You will see love where you did not see it before. You will see love in the people that you thought were your enemies. When you believe that all things happen for a reason and believe that all things are connected to the Source, you see messages all around you.

The day I wrote this page I left my office at noon and went to the local store to buy food for lunch. Once or twice each week I do this because it allows me to get out of the office during the busy day and think about what really matters in my life. What is really happening is that the intelligence and energy of the Source is living and experiencing life all around me and I don't want to lose sight of this truth. I realize the Source is all around and in all the people at the store. Even though they may not be aware of it, they are the physical manifestation of the Source.

Today as I pulled into the parking lot, I had a feeling to park in a different part of the lot than I normally do. There was no reason to do this other than I simply felt a strong message telling me to park at the opposite end of the lot from where I normally park. I've been to this store a hundred times and I have never parked where I was urged to park today.

As I walked to the door, I saw an older man coming out pushing a cart, being followed by a store employee pushing his second cart of groceries. As he walked down the sloping sidewalk ramp he fell, landing face down flat on the concrete. The store employee was so upset she let go of the cart and ran toward the man, squatted down, and asked him if he was all right. Meanwhile the abandoned cart was rolling down the slope toward the man's head.

I was only twenty feet away and I ran over to stop the cart from hitting the man; then I helped him stand up. After making sure he was all right, I proceeded to pick up the food which had fallen out of the bags. The store employee was obviously upset and wanted to get another employee to help. I told her I was glad to help pick up the food and walk the man to his car. Immediately I understood why I heard the voice tell me to park on that side of the parking lot that day.

The message does not need to be profound or life shaking. The Source sends messages on many levels, sometimes on important issues, sometimes to guide you toward a particular experience. The point is that every aspect of life happens intentionally, and the Source is constantly showing you things to learn. If you become accustomed to listening to it and following its direction, you will usually see why it guides you the way it does. Practice allows you to hear better and more clearly.

Some people use tools to help them hear the messages. You can find messages through numerology, astrology, palm reading, and other practices. Some people who proclaim they have power to do these things are pretenders. However, many sincere people have the knowledge and ability to connect with the Source and use these tools to help them see the picture more clearly. Most will tell you they can find the answers inside themselves without tools or aids, but the aids help them do it faster or with more clarity.

When you don't believe everything comes from a Source and is still connected to it, things such as numerology make no sense. When you believe everything is part of the Source, you can see these tools as expressions of creation and of yourself. While you live in this world where the illusion is powerful, these tools help you see reality more clearly.

The Play of Life

Life is like a play that has been written but not yet acted out on stage. You are an actor who has agreed to come to earth and act a certain role. Some people have chosen fun roles and others have chosen difficult roles. Imagine that you are asked to act in a play for one full day. You are told that the other people in the play will not know this is a play; they will believe it is real life.

Since you know this is only a play, you perform the role without allowing yourself to become stressed. No matter what the circumstances of the play, you do not become emotionally hurt or experience the anger, fear, and jealousy of the character. It is easy for you to have fun with the play no matter what happens because you know it is not real. You know that when the play is over, life will continue without being influenced negatively by anything in the play.

Other people in the play don't know it is just a play; they believe it is real. The other actors are serious about the events of the play because it is real to them. When they bargain for a pay raise, for instance, they are emotionally stressed.

You know that some people will never learn this is a play. They will live with the consequences of the play for years. Whatever pain you inflict into their lives in the play will last them a lifetime. The anger you generate in them will remain a part of them and their families for years. You are in a unique situation because you realize this is just a play, but they don't know it and they may not know it for many years.

This illustration is a powerful way to view your life. The script is written for your life and you are acting it out as if in a play. Along the way you improvise and choose many of the lines you say and the things you do. It does not matter so much what happens, but rather how you respond to situations. It does not matter how wealthy you become, but rather how you acquire such wealth. It does not matter how poor you are, but how you respond to being poor. It matters how you impact other people's lives. What seeds have you planted during your lifetime? Do you help others when you can or do you tell others to help themselves even when they cannot?

Even though you know you have a role in this play of life, you may forget at times that it is just a play. Remember that before this play started you were united with the Source, but once the play started you forgot everything. Part of the experience of life is to find your way back to the Source — to find your way back to knowing who you are. This is sometimes called "awakening" or being "enlightened."

Because your identity was hidden at birth, the purpose of life is to recover that identity. It is not up to you to decide when the time is right for others to find themselves. They will find themselves when the time is right for them. It is more important how you *respond* to the fact that they have not yet found what you have found.

Do not try to force others into your way of thinking. Trust that the Source inside them will become known to them at the exact time it is supposed to. Their plan is likely different from yours.

Your Choices

Now you must choose what to believe. You have read in the previous two sections about the common beliefs people find when they search within themselves and connect with their Source. It is up to you to go through this process to find your own inspired beliefs to make your life feel whole and good.

The past is not now.

The future does not exist.

The present makes what is

and influences what will be.

CHAPTER 5

Live in the Present

This chapter addresses living in the present moment of time and why it is important. This is *Step Five* of the **Ten Steps to Finding the Secret Inside**.

Ten Steps to Finding the Secret Inside

1. Understand your current perception
2. Heal your emotional pain
3. Look inside yourself
4. Choose new beliefs
5. ***Live in the present***
6. Find creative power within you
7. Be emotionally aware
8. Align your personality
9. Embrace what "Is"
10. Transcend the illusion

"The Present" Defined

Living in the present is focusing your attention on the current moment of time. It means you think about what is happening now rather than thinking about the past or the future. It means you make plans now based on what is happening, rather than based on what happened in the past. Much of life is wasted not living in the present. This chapter shows why living in the present is necessary to be happy.

The idea of time is only a concept created in your mind to categorize the events of your life. Now is the only real event. You can show me now by saying "Here it is" as you extend your arms and point to the world around you. But, you cannot show me the past and you cannot show me the future. Now is happening, the past is not happening, and the future is not happening. Memories of your past are only able to be recalled *now*. Without you being here, now, you could not remember the past.

When you live in the present it's not productive to worry about the future and not practical to fume about the past. Neither past nor future exist in the window of the present; they are only thoughts in your mind *now*. This is not to say you didn't experience past events. Rather, there is no substance to those past events other than the memories you cling to.

The present is where all things happen to you. Now, you are sitting reading this book. You are concentrating on the words and paying attention to their meaning. By doing this, you are focused in the present. But there is more to the present than simply being focused on what is happening to you.

The present also represents the window in space and time where all creation is manifest. The entire universe cannot be seen because it is infinite and unlimited. Infinite love cannot be seen. Infinite anything cannot be seen. In order for you to experience the universe, a window of time and space must be made for the events of your life to be created and experienced. This is the present moment. It is the window in which your life is lived. It is this point of singularity where all things are created. It is this moment when you have the clarity to direct the activities of your life to become exactly what you want them to be. There is no other place where your life exists except in this single moment of time called "the present."

Why You Might Not Live in the Present

Much of life is wasted not living in the present for two reasons. First, you might not realize who you are, and because of that you attempt to protect the false sense of self. Secondly, you might be looking for happiness, but, by not understanding that it is only found in the present, you look for it in the past or the future.

Living with your mind in the past or the future is counter-productive because it reinforces the illusion, the false sense of a separate self. When you believe the illusion, you believe you can be hurt; you envision ways to protect and defend yourself. You may even waste time thinking about the future, rehearsing ways to defend yourself during an anticipated confrontation.

The reason you spend time thinking about the past or the future is because you see yourself, not as a part of the energy of the universe, but as a person separate from everything else in the universe. If you experienced moments of joy in the past, you will likely want to re-create those experiences in your mind. But by doing so, you maintain the illusion that you are separate from your Source and you retain only a memory of joy rather than creating joy right now.

If a past experience was one of pain, anger, or difficulty, you re-live it, feeling sorry for yourself because you believed you needed to be cared for and others would not care for you. This is harmful because it promotes the false image of you as disconnected from your Source. The truth is that the illusion of you being separate from your Source is the sole cause of your pain and suffering. By dwelling on the past you cling to baggage that will continue to bring you adversity and struggles.

Take heart! The true you is your inner self, your Source, which cannot be hurt. You are a divine being living a human life, so why waste time contemplating how to protect the illusion? This behavior promotes the false illusion of who you think you are; it is detrimental. When you worry about future events and imagine problematic situations, you often set into motion the creation of those very things you fear.

Memories of good times also are not healthy if they are outside the present moment. Recollections of "the good old days" reinforce past events that encouraged the ego: love affairs, feelings of importance, times when you felt adored when you were in the spotlight. Those memories contribute to the impression of a separate self needing to be loved. This is not in balance with who you are. You are a divine being. You do not require love from others because love originates inside you; you produce love for yourself and for others. When you know that you are love, you project it to yourself and to the world.

Another way you might squander your time is by waiting ineffectively. Sound familiar? On a small scale you wait in line at the grocery store, you wait to get your driver license renewed, and you wait in traffic jams. During those times, if you only focus on getting to where you want to go, you are wasting precious moments of your life. While waiting in traffic, rather than regard it a hindrance, consider that you were supposed to be trapped in traffic. Consider it a good time to rest your mind and tap into the consciousness of the Source inside you. Use each moment to connect with your Source. Where you are heading on your commute is not important, but connecting with your Source is.

On a larger scale you might be postponing your happiness by thinking that it can only arrive some time in the future. You might create thoughts like these:

I'll be happy when the week-end arrives.
I'll be happy when I get a vacation.
I'll be happy when I make more money.
I'll be happy when I find a partner.
I'll be happy when I can afford my own house.
I'll be happy when I get married.
I'll be happy when I have children.
I'll be happy when we can afford a larger house.
I'll be happy when the children leave home.
I'll be happy when I can retire.
I'll be happy when I divorce and find another partner.
I'll be happy when we downsize to a smaller house.
I'll be happy when I get to heaven.

All these events are only thoughts of the illusion you hold in your mind about how to find happiness. None of them take place in the present, and therefore none of them can ever become reality because reality occurs in the present moment.

Examine your thoughts for a moment and take inventory of the type of thinking you do. If your attention is on reading these words, you are living in the present moment. But, if you have ever found yourself reading words while your mind thinks about something else, then those are the times, you aren't living in the present moment.

In the morning, while getting ready for the day, is your mind available to enjoy the act of showering, brushing teeth and dressing, or do you think about the day ahead of you and all the tasks that need to be accomplished?

Do you enjoy eating breakfast? Do you think about the food you put into your body and savor how it tastes? Or do you gobble down your food like a hungry animal? While you eat in your kitchen is your mind already at work thinking about the responsibilities of the day?

As you leave your house, do you step outside and smell the air you breathe? Do you smell flowers? Do you see the sunlight and enjoy the heat it makes on your face? Do you sense the breeze blowing on your hands and face? Do you notice the freshness of the rain? Do you detect the briskness of the air?

Do you live in the present moment, or do you live with your mind anticipating the future? When you drive, do you watch the road and glance at the sky and grass and trees, or is your mind imagining the events of the day ahead?

Examine the state of your mind during your free time. Do those near you ever tell you that even though you are physically present, you are not really *present* because your mind is somewhere else? When you arrive at a destination, do you not remember the details of the drive because your mind was busy and your body went on auto pilot?

While lying in bed at night, does your mind run uncontrolled, thinking about either past or future conversations or events? You might be worried about an interview, a personal confrontation, a difficult job, or any number of things.

An enormous amount of living is wasted when you are not present in the only place where life is happening. All life is created in the present. You have no way to prove that the future will ever happen. You can only be sure that *now* is happening, and now is the only thing you can control.

There is a cost to not living in the present moment. The most obvious is that you miss experiencing your divinity. There is a journey of life unfolding before your eyes and you miss it when you don't live in the present moment. Eternity is not to be found in the hereafter. Eternity is what is happening right now. You are a creative being with the ability to influence life as it happens. You cannot direct your life when you are re-living the past or too busy worrying about the future.

How to Live in the Present

Live in the present by focusing your mind on what is happening right now. Whenever you notice yourself recalling memories or thinking about the future, stop and bring yourself back to think about who you are now and what you desire for your life. Resist letting your mind squander time on memories, particularly of sorrow or of great joy. These types of thoughts create strong bonds with the false self of your ego, not your true self who is one with the Source.

What you create now will become tomorrow's reality. For example: if you want to start your own business, now is the time to create it. You cannot wait for the future to create your life because the future is not where everything exists; the future is only a thought, not actuality. If you want a new reality for your career, take action now and devise a plan and implement it.

It's okay to plan for the future as long as you are not waiting to get there. Waiting is a state of mind that causes unhappiness. Just because you don't yet have something you desire doesn't mean you need to wait and be unhappy until you get it. You can plan for it and then begin acting immediately. You will then be purposefully creating life, now, to be what you want it to be.

There is wonderful joy in choosing to live and act in the present moment. Choose right now to:

Call a friend
Buy a new book
Change your attitude
Speak kind words to others
Connect with the Source inside you
See purpose in everything
Be whatever you want
Be happy
Exercise
Be rich
Be free

Most unhappiness exists when you are not living in the present. Most of the time you really don't need all the things you think you need, and you don't need to be as unhappy as you feel. With that in mind, answer the following questions.

1. Do you need to feel hurt?
2. Do you need more money?
3. Do you need to wait to make your life what you want it to be?
4. Do you need to remember all your bad memories?
5. Do you need to keep all the limitations others placed on you?
6. Do you need to associate with the people that don't make you feel good?
7. Do you need more possessions to make you happy?
8. Do you need people to like you for you to be happy?
9. Do you need to be afraid?

The answers are all no. You do not need any of those things to make you happy, and none of them can ever make you happy. All happiness is found in knowing you are a part of the energy (Source) that made all things, and by living in the only space of time that exists, called *now*.

Your memories don't need to influence your future. Memories about your life are only thoughts you held onto before you knew you were part of your Source, or they were thoughts caused by what other people said about you.

For example, in your past you might remember feeling inadequate for not having the education you wanted. In reality, this is the life you created for yourself. It was supposed to happen exactly that way. The proof of that is because it did happen that way. You now have the complete power to change your reality if you don't like it. If you want to become more educated, choose to research and find opportunities for education. Announce your plans to friends and family and begin believing it is a new life for you. If you sincerely believe it, it will come about and if you are willing to work and take action, it will become your new reality.

Perhaps you are broke. If you want to change that reality, believe you can change it and take action now. Just because you were that way in the past has nothing to do with what you can create for your future.

Maybe you have failed to be successful at something. The failure brought pain. Now, because you fear more failure, you don't take more risks. You believe you can be hurt again and worry another failure will validate the fear that you are inadequate. If this is the case, you've let this incorrect belief from the past stop you from being something wonderful now and in your future. Instead, you need to create a new belief in the present moment where you know you will be successful at whatever it is you wish for. Set a plan and start to work today to bring about that plan, without waiting for it.

In the past you might have experienced hurts from relationships with parents, children, family, or friends. You remember those hurts and do not want to feel them again. Because of this you alter what you do now in a way that limits your total freedom and happiness. You let your past hurts prevent you from being something divinely great today and in your future — all because you believe you were hurt and that you can be hurt again.

The truth is that you are a part of the place where love originates, a place where no hurt exists. Therefore, you do not lack love; you are the creator of all love for both you and others. Start to change by loving yourself more than anything else in the world. You will never ever be able to feel love until you create love for yourself. To do this, believe that you are a part of the Source. This is where all love comes from. When you believe this, you can experience love like nothing else in this world. It will overflow to others and come flowing back to you.

Some people live life by keeping their minds mired in the past. This is like driving a car while looking out the back window. You can't see where your life takes you, and you miss opportunities and adventures because you are looking behind you.

To drive your life, you need to be present. You need to sit in the car to steer it while looking out the front window. You need to be looking ahead and deciding where you want to go. To make something a reality, believe in it and plan for it. However, that alone will not get you there. You will only get there if you *drive* the car. Driving the car means you take action now in your life to bring about what you want it to be.

Live your life by accepting what comes and planning for everything you want to come. Then act to make it happen. Accept all that happens because it is what you previously set into motion, whether you like it or not. It is supposed to happen; search for the meaning in it. Decide what you want your life to be and take action now. Realize it takes time to physically manifest itself, but believe that it is already here.

When you live in the present moment you have clarity to project onto your life the things you want. By doing so, you begin the process of creation. Creation is bringing into existence things or events that you desire, things not currently in your life. You must be in the *present* moment to create your life.

When you spend time in the past or future rather than in the present moment, your physical health suffers. You fail to take advantage of healthy living — things such as breathing, eating, sleeping, relaxing, exercising, meditating, and thinking positive thoughts about the present moment.

Spending most of your time in past or future states of mind is unhealthy for your psychological health. This type of thinking is usually associated with stressful emotions of worry, anger, frustration, jealousy, need, or fear. These emotions manifest themselves negatively in the body and cause all forms of diseases.

Instead of living in the past or future, live in the present, outside the illusion, where you understand that the purpose of your life is to re-discover your Source connection. You'll see the world as good and you'll start to see how to make it even better.

What you can imagine,

you can create.

Otherwise, you would not

have imagined it.

<hr>

CHAPTER 6

Find Creative Power Within You

This chapter shows how to create your life to be the way you want it. This is *Step Six* of the **Ten Steps to Finding the Secret Inside**.

Ten Steps to Finding the Secret Inside
1. Understand your current perception
2. Heal your emotional pain
3. Look inside yourself
4. Choose new beliefs
5. Live in the present
6. ***Find creative power within you***
7. Be emotionally aware
8. Align your personality
9. Embrace what "Is"
10. Transcend the illusion

Creation is one of the most powerful things you can experience. You have the ability to create joy, good health, wealth, and every detail of your life. Most religions say all things were created out of one Source. Since you are a part of that Source, you have the same creative ability inside you.

You are the physical manifestation of the Source. Just as your body has many parts, so does the Source. Your mind is the thinking part of your body. You are the conscious thinking part of the Source. You are the part of Source which has consciousness, the ability to act and make miracles. You do this through a process called creation.

Cause and Effect

You've heard the conundrum, "Which came first, the chicken or the egg?" One is a cause and the other an effect. Life is full of cause and effect. Creation uses the principles of cause and effect to bring about what you want. You will not find fulfillment in your life until you understand the principles of creation and of cause and effect.

You may believe your life circumstances cause you to feel the way you do. This is an erroneous perception, the opposite of the truth. Your thoughts and feelings bring about your life circumstances. You first think it and feel it; then you encounter it. You attract everything into your life that is there. Your thinking initiates the creation of situations in your life. The situations are the effects of your thinking. Change your thinking and you will change what you create for your life.

Read the last two sentences again to grasp their significance.

The Beginning

The Source contains all consciousness and all matter and all energy. This idea of all things being in one place at one time is the concept of the Source before creation.

Creation began when you (the Source) decided to evolve and improve yourself. You began improving yourself by splitting into many parts; that became the creation. Some parts became living matter, some non-living matter; some became feelings, some electromagnetic energy; some became ideas, and others became abstract concepts.

The purpose of the separation was for you (the Source) to interact with others and to allow learning to occur. In this way you (the Source) could evolve and improve. Pieces cannot be seen as individual parts until they are separated and contrasted with each other. The separation allows you to experience love and fear, hot and cold, light and dark as individual parts, even though you know all things are connected in the oneness of the Source.

When the earth was created it likely evolved over millions and billions of years, and possibly forever. The Source is represented in each part of creation, yet each part contains the whole Source. Each part remains connected to the whole and retains the full knowledge and abilities of the whole. One of those abilities is the power to bring things into existence. You are a part of that Source and are connected to the whole Source. You have the ability to create, just as you did when you/Source created all things.

If you believe this, now is the time to exclaim, "WOW!"

Principles of Creation (Desire, Belief, Exchange, Action)

There are principles in the universe that describe how the

universe works, things such as gravity, light, and energy. The universe does not make these principles; the universe simply operates according to them. People find ways to explain the universe by formulating principles which describe what they see happening. Today science focuses mostly on the natural laws relating to physical matter and energy. Over the last two centuries, scientists have realized that there are powerful energy forces which are not visible, things such as electromagnetic energy.

The next frontier in knowledge will be when science uncovers the natural laws of the yet unseen realm of creation. Eventually people will come to realize that all things in the universe are connected by a fabric of energy woven through all matter and through all ideas, spirit, and concepts; it is the energy of the Source, the stuff from which we are all made. This will be the universal law that describes all things in one simple definition. Today science is looking for that universal law. It is on track with one theory called the "String Theory."

String Theory states that all things in the universe are composed of strings of energy. Every string vibrates a different way and expands or shrinks to different configurations. All strings are identical, but they vibrate differently. These vibrational differences are what determine how energy is manifest. Some energy is manifest in physical matter, some in light, and some in electromagnetic energy. Therefore you are made of the same energy as light. The only difference is how your strings of energy vibrate differently from the strings of light. When we understand how to control and change energy, we will be able to transform ourselves and everything else into whatever we choose.

A principle which is not yet recognized by science, but one which has been operating in the universe since the beginning, is that of creation. Creation is the process of transforming your own energy into another form through the power of your thoughts. The universe and all that exists is the result of this principle.

The universe is expanding; nature creates through life and death and re-birth; people create every moment of every day whether they are conscious of it or not.

When you have knowledge of the miracle that you are part of the Source, it is not difficult to believe in your power to create. By connecting with your Source you set into motion the creation of what you desire.

There are four principles of creation. When you understand how they work, you can use them to produce the results you want.

In my life I've created peace, happiness, good health, wealth, and many more things. My writing career was set into motion when one day in meditation I was inspired to write this book. I had never published anything. I chose to set into motion a book that would reach many people throughout the world. To do this, I needed to create a great book along with a large-scale marketing effort to promote it. The result is the creation of books, websites, speaking engagements, and more. By doing this, I set into motion the creation of something I love to do. And as it becomes effective, I can spend my time moving toward what I was meant to be and sharing with others how they can become what they were meant to be.

1. First Principle of Creation: Desire

The first principle of creation is Desire. Desire comes from the consciousness of the Source, which is in you. It does not come from a human body or a human brain; it comes from the Source inside you, which lives forever.

When you live in the illusion of not knowing who you are, you identify a lot of things you want, but fail to know how to bring those things into existence. The principle of Creation works to create things every day, but you may not know how it works. Therefore, you are not controlling what is being created. When you don't understand what is happening, you create circumstances in your life that you don't like and then wonder why they occur.

Everyone has the ability to create. The problem is that people fail to do it in a way that produces a desired result. It is similar to the apprentice magician who has magical powers but fails to produce the right spells at the right times. There is no question as to the power of the apprentice, but the power is worthless if it cannot be focused to create the desired results at the right time.

Desire must be powerful, an obsession. Those who are obsessed with something think about it all the time; they daydream about it, they dream at night about it. They imagine how life would be once they obtain it. This level of desire is required because the amount of time spent thinking about the chosen outcome is what sends energy to the universe to set into motion the creation of your desires.

If you wanted to become physically fit, you would exercise more than one time. You would probably establish a daily exercise routine where you exercise more than just one minute per day. You know that the level of your physical fitness is proportionate to the amount of time you spend exercising. Creation is the same way. When you desire something for your life, you cannot think about it one time and hope it will arrive. You must think about it often. Spend a regular part of every day envisioning your desired result.

Know it is already on its way. Dream of what the details of your life will be when it has arrived. Desire it every moment of your life.

This is the level of desire that must exist for you to create anything you want with your thoughts. For that reason, you should create only those things that you love. Desire the things that you want to do or be for the rest of your life. Desire is only the first ingredient of the creation process.

2. Second Principle of Creation: Belief

The second principle of creation is belief. You must believe you can create the thing you want. You must believe it can be done and believe that you have the *sole* power to bring it into existence.

If you ever wished to be a millionaire you are like many people. Most people believe it is possible, but most also believe it is not likely to happen to them. Their belief of becoming a millionaire is weak, but their belief that they won't become a millionaire is strong. Belief like this will not create what you want. Something else besides what you want will be created because the law of creation is always producing results based on your strongest belief.

In the illustration above, the desired result is to become a millionaire, but the belief that it will happen is weak. Your stronger belief is that you will never become a millionaire. Your strongest belief sets into motion the creation of whatever that belief is, ensuring that you will never become a millionaire.

Therefore, the first principle of creation requires an idea to be generated in your mind of something you desire. The second principle requires you to believe with all your heart that you can and will bring it into existence by the very act of creating it in your mind. This is creation at work, but it is incomplete without the next two principles.

3. Third Principle of Creation: Exchange

The third principle of creation is exchange. The universe is always in balance. If you want something, you must be willing to exchange something for it.

Give something beneficial to the world in exchange for what you desire in your life. Give something meaningful and helpful. Give your time, your ideas, your love, your goods, your services, or something else.

What you give does not need to be equal in value to the reward you wish to receive. Nature shows that when you plant a small seed it grows to produce a crop a hundred or thousand times larger than what was planted.

In the same way, give seeds to the world. You can give ideas, time, goods, and labor. Over time these grow into great value for the world. You can request rewards of a thousand or million times that which you planted.

You do not need to give one million dollars in value in order to reap one million dollars. Plant seeds of things that people want or need, things that will make the world a better place. Goodness has more value than money, so a little goodness is worth more than a lot of money.

Creation starts with your *desire*. Then you must *believe* you can create it, and you must offer a reasonable *exchange* between you and the universe, describing what you will give in return for what you want to create.

4. Fourth Principle of Creation: Action

The final law of creation is to act upon your belief. A farmer *desires* a large crop and *believes* in the ability to make it become a reality. Although willing to *exchange* money to buy the seed, failure to take *action* and plant the seeds will ensure that no creation occurs. You must make plans to act and then follow through with those plans in order to bring about your creation.

When I was given the idea to write this book I had a lot of reasons not to do it. I had no training to write. I didn't know anyone who wrote professionally. I had a full-time job in a field unrelated to writing.

However, in meditation I became inspired to begin a career built around what I love. I love learning about the Source inside me, allowing me to create peace, love, and freedom. I became inspired to give my life to developing this in myself and encouraging others to find it in themselves. I was given the idea and the desire to create it in my life. I believed I would make it happen. I knew I would exchange my time and energy to write for however long it took. I was willing to write and write again. I was willing to fail over and over again.

I knew the challenges ahead might include failure, failure to find an agent, failure with publishing houses, failure with bookstores, failure with marketing attempts, and failure with public speaking. But I knew these were only minor setbacks in the journey to success. I knew that most successes come at the expense of many failures. I was willing to fail many times and keep going, because I believed it would become reality. I was willing to invest my money and time into the endeavor of publishing and speaking about something that will improve people's lives.

I was willing to pay a large price to complete this process, no different than a farmer who must work long and hard toiling in the soil, plowing, seeding, and cultivating. I was willing to pay a price, and in exchange I would ask for a return. I made a deal with the universe that I will do this in return for two things: knowledge and financial freedom. First, I want my writing efforts to bring me increased knowledge. Dedication to writing books requires me to connect with my Source for the words to write and ideas to share. In this way I gain immense knowledge.

Secondly, I desire financial freedom so I can focus on what is most important to me in this journey of life. I want to spend my time doing what I love most, seeking personal growth and sharing it with others. Using the principles of creation, I've set into motion my desire. It became a reality in my mind.

I knew I would write this book and others; I had imagined it; I believed it would happen. I made an exchange with the universe. Next I needed to act. Without this final step, nothing could happen. Without this step, the principle of creation would continue to operate not according to what I wanted, but according to my actions.

If I failed to begin the writing process and instead opted to watch television, my actions would have set into motion a new direction for creation to manifest. Creation would not manifest a successful book, but would simply make me more informed about television shows and make my body get out of shape from sitting on the couch too much. Action is simply another extension of belief. Action is the demonstration of belief.

Jesus found the God within him and used the principles of creation. People came to him requesting that he heal them. All the people he healed had to first demonstrate their complete belief before any miracle could occur. Some had to walk a long way to get to him; others had to open up a roof of a house where he was speaking to gain access to him.

A blind man had to allow Jesus to spit in the mud and smear mud in the man's eyes. A man with leprosy had to dip into the dirty Jordan River seven times. Those actions were required of the people wanting the reward of healing. They demonstrated their beliefs.

One man wanted to have the power that Jesus had and asked what he must do to get it. Jesus told him he must sell all his possessions and give the money to the poor. This action would have demonstrated that the man believed he could re-create his own wealth. But when he failed to believe that he would be able to re-create it, he was not willing to sell his possessions. Action is a demonstration of your belief, and it must be done for the law of creation to become complete. Jesus used this law and taught it to twelve of his disciples who learned the process thoroughly enough to perform many miracles. Creation today is no different.

As I wrote this portion of the book I was sitting in an RV motor home with my son and our dog. We had taken a two-week trip across many states to see Zion National Park, the Grand Canyon, a friend in Las Vegas, the desert, San Francisco, and the California Coast. That morning we left Morro Bay near San Luis Obisbo, California and headed north up the coast.

Each day we normally started out by filling up the gas tank. That morning the gas tank was only one-quarter full and I consciously decided not to fill it at the gas station nearby. I drove past without stopping; it was a conscious decision that made no logical sense because we were heading up Highway 1 along the California coast where I knew there are no gas stations. My son asked as we drove past the station if we should stop and fill up, but I said no, we would be okay. Something inside compelled me not to stop.

As we drove along the winding coast road, the gas gauge dropped below one quarter and was heading toward the empty mark. My son asked several times if we should have gotten gas. At first I said we would make it all the way to the next big town, but soon realized that we would not make it. We had been driving a long time with nothing in sight except coast line — no country store, no town, not even a house. We were traveling along narrow roads built into the cliff rising from the ocean.

I knew we could not make it back to the last town and I knew we could not make it to the next town, and it appeared there was not going to be any gas station along the way. I realized we would run out of gas. At that moment I became inspired with an idea. I realized the Source that made the universe could surely create anything, even a gas station out in the middle of nowhere. And I knew this Source was in me and I was a part of it.

I turned to my twelve-year-old son and asked if we should practice the laws of creation to make a gas station right here in the middle of nowhere. My son asked if we could really do that and agreed to try. I explained that if I believed I can create a gas station and have complete belief, it will surely come into existence. My explanation took about one minute. I told my son that I would meditate for a moment to set the energy into motion to create a gas station ahead of us. At that moment I believed completely, without a doubt, that this was possible.

Fifteen seconds later we turned a corner and there was a small lodge, small stores, and a gas station. My son said, "Wow."

I explained that this was a result of us creating with the power of thought and belief. My son questioned how we could have created the gas station when it appeared it was old and obviously had been there more than fifteen seconds. It had the look of an established area, not one that had just been created by me only fifteen seconds earlier. The people who worked there were real people with real lives; they had lived for many years.

We are not only physical people, but also spiritual beings which operate outside the dimensions of time and space. When we meditate in the present moment, we can affect things in the past and in the future. When I went into the store I asked how long it had been there. I was told that a man and wife retired in 1962 and decided to settle there and build a store, a small inn, and a gas station. When I had meditated in the present moment, my intention joined forces with the intention of a couple living in 1962 when they got the idea to build in this very spot. My energy joined with theirs to create it at the very spot I needed.

It is not important to me that the gas station was built in 1962, but the location is important because I needed it to be exactly there. My creative power influenced bringing a gas station into existence at the exact location I needed it to be. If I had chosen to wait another ten minutes before I meditated, then the gas station would not have been located in that spot, but rather ten minutes farther down the road. I know that.

Why? Because my creative power would have joined with a couple living in 1962 who was contemplating the location for those buildings and my intention would have influenced their decision to locate the station ten minutes farther up the road.

Afterwards, I understood why I had acted out of character when I chose not to get gas that morning. The Source inside prompted me to act out of character in order to experience the power of creation on the very day that I was writing this chapter. My exchange with the universe is to include this story to inspire you.

Even though I believed the book would become reality, I asked myself the question: what must happen for a book to become real? Words had to be written. I had to write a lot. I had to organize my ideas and organize chapters. I had to learn the book publishing process.

This is the action I put forth to bring this book into creation. This is what I was willing to give the universe in exchange for my desires so I could spend time doing what I love best.

How To Create Peace

People spend a lot of time chasing money because they think it will quell the unsatisfied desire within them. People don't really want money; they want happiness and contentment, which they think money brings.

How do you use the process of creation to bring happiness and contentment? Apply the four principles of creation and create it as beautifully as you desire!

First use your imagination to visualize a life of happiness and contentment, not needing love from others, not needing possessions or money, not needing status and fame. Figure out what it is you desire in your life. Nothing is wrong with riches and fame, but they won't bring peace. Imagine your life to be content and happy — peaceful.

Imagine the details of what you want for your life. Imagine people around you who love you and respect you. Imagine you are able to relax, that you have time to meditate, time to rest, time to exercise, time to enjoy eating healthy. Imagine not needing to work unless you want to work. Imagine being able to travel the world and meet all kinds of people and see different cultures. Imagine having unlimited wealth for whatever you desire.

The second step is to believe beyond a doubt that you have within you the sole power to bring this into existence. If you find it difficult, you have not accepted the fact that you are part of the Source from which everything came. You must know that you are the Source who envisions things and you are the Source who acts to bring them into existence.

If you don't believe you are part of the Source, then you will never find peace because you are looking for peace outside yourself. Peace does not exist there. Peace comes through knowing you are one with the Source which is found inside you. The power to create ideas is within you and the ability to turn those ideas into reality is inside you.

If your belief is weak, start the process by thinking of small things to create that you do have faith to believe in. Consider believing you will find a parking stall close to the front door of the store. Consider believing you will find a sale for something you need. Consider that you can start a club or a group that you have wanted to establish. Begin the creative process at whatever level you have faith to believe. It will work only if you have complete confidence that you can create it.

For the third principle, be willing to exchange something for what you want. You must be willing to give your time, your ideas, your belief, and your effort. You must offer something to others in order to get what you want; it is an exchange. Sometimes I ask for a parking stall close to the front door; in exchange, I offer to intentionally look for someone in that store to help. I look for a person who needs the door held open, or for someone to smile at, or for someone who needs a helping hand, or someone to say hello to. This is a simple exchange of kindness for a parking stall close to the front door; it works.

The fourth principle of creation requires you to act in order to bring about the creation. If you want peace in your life, work to create that peace. How do you do that? You must realize that love and peace do not come from the outside. You are Peace and Love. You are a part of the Source where all things originate. Meditate daily on this fact. Meditate on the truth that you are divine and that within you is all the love and peace of the universe. You produce it.

Extend peace and love to everyone around you. Plant seeds of goodness. The seeds you plant grow into a crop a thousand or million times larger than what you plant.

The principles of creation are in continual operation. Everything you think sets into motion the physical manifestation of those thoughts. Each time you get angry you plant a seed that will bring into existence the opposite of your desire for peace. Therefore resist anger.

How do you resist anger when people offend you? You resist it by remembering that you cannot be hurt. You will not feel pain unless you believe in the illusion that you are separate from the Source. When you believe you are separate, you set into motion that reality, causing you to feel pain. When you feel pain, change your belief to see yourself as part of the Source which cannot be hurt.

Each day of living you have the wonderful opportunity to create whatever you choose by implementing the four principles of creation. Over time you can create anything, even a new world of peace. The world you have created has come about over millions of years by the acts of people creating it into being. What you see now is the result of these past creations. What do you want for tomorrow?

How to Create Wealth

Creating wealth is no different than creating other things, but it is more popular and sought after. People who know the secret of the miracle inside can create anything they want or can become anything they desire; they can be or can create things such as:

Fame

Wealth

An artist

A musician

A spouse

A parent

World peace

Personal peace

Good health

A best-selling author

Freedom to travel the world

A grandparent

A television show

A new house

A new car

A gas station when needed

Everything you can imagine that you want to create is simply an idea. All things that already exist are ideas that have become manifest into existence. Money is no different; money is just an idea. Money itself is not a tangible item. The paper dollar is only a note representing the idea of money. A check is only an idea representing something of value. Credit cards are pieces of plastic and represent only an idea of value. Bank statements are pieces of paper that represent ideas of value. Money is only an idea.

A one dollar bill costs the same to produce as a ten dollar bill. The only difference between them is the idea. Similarly, a check can be written for a value of five dollars or one million dollars. The two checks look similar, but the idea of one is worth much more than the idea of the other.

Money is an idea. Ideas generate and create money. Remember, the principles of creation start with ideas and desire. Ideas generate all wealth. Wealth is unlimited because there is no limit to how many ideas you can generate.

If you think money is limited, you are mistaken. Ideas generate money as fast as people can think up new ideas to create it. Fifty years ago who would have imagined that a company could make money selling bottles of water? This occurs even where people have access to the purest tap water, which is free.

People generated an idea to create an internet garage sale called EBAY.com where people all over the world can sell new or used items to anyone around the world. What an idea. People who created wealth from this followed the principles of creation. They generated an idea, they believed it could be accomplished, they agreed how it would bring value to the world, and they acted to create it.

Other people generated an idea of creating a search engine

to help find anything you want on the Internet. They believed it could work, they believed it brought value to the world, and they acted to bring it into existence. They generated significant amounts of wealth in the process.

Financial freedom is really not about money, it is about the idea of abundance. When you learn the principles of creation, you realize that all things can be abundant because you are part of the Source that can bring into existence anything you desire. When you think that the world has a limited supply of money and you want to have a lot of it, you are greedy. But when you know that the amount of money is unlimited, you are not greedy even if you desire to accumulate a lot of it. You will never be happy if you think you need money to be happy. But, once you know how to be happy, creating a lot of money can be helpful in accomplishing what you want.

Greed only exists when you believe something is scarce and you do not want to share it. When something is as unlimited and abundant as the air, there is no selfishness in wanting to breathe a lot of it. The same is true with money. Once you know that money is unlimited and that everyone has the ability to create it in unlimited amounts, it is not selfish to create a lot of it for good use. It is similar to producing happiness or love. There is no such thing as greed when you want to produce huge amounts of happiness and love for yourself and others. Money is the same way once you realize it is as unlimited as the ideas in your mind and as unlimited as the air you breathe.

If you want to establish wealth you only need to implement the laws of creation. You can generate ideas to write, paint, develop real estate, make movies, start businesses, help children, raise horses, heal people, or millions of other things. Any of these things can bring wealth if the principles of creation are executed.

There is no other formula to define success at attaining wealth. I have worked with dozens of multi-millionaires during my career. I have witnessed people making many millions of dollars on each deal they execute while others doing the same work go bankrupt.

Some people take excessive risks and win. Other people take excessive risks and lose. Some people make conservative business decisions and make millions. Other people make conservative business decisions and go bankrupt. Some honest people win and become multi-millionaires, while other honest people lose everything they own. Some selfish people win and become multi-millionaires and other selfish people lose out.

The formula for financial success is not dependent upon the things most people have believed it to be. If it were, you would see a very obvious trend leading to financial success. Below is a list of false beliefs people have about getting rich.

False Beliefs About How To Get Rich

- ✦ Be conservative
- ✦ Take risk
- ✦ Know the right people
- ✦ Be in the right place at the right time
- ✦ Have the right education
- ✦ Obtain the right job
- ✦ Live in the right economic time
- ✦ Practice a good moral life
- ✦ Learn to bend the rules (cheat)
- ✦ Be born into a wealthy family

+ Maintain an image of wealth and status
+ Be smart
+ Become a workaholic
+ Get lucky
+ Marry into wealth

Many people are not aware of how wealth is created. It is not necessarily related to education, or risk taking, or being conservative with money, or having a good moral character, or anything else listed above. Financial success may accompany any one or more of these items, but those are not the reason why wealth gets created.

Wealth is created when the principles of creation are used to create it. People create ideas to bring value to the world and develop strong desires to do something that brings about wealth. When they implement the principles of creation, people pay for the products or use the services, and wealth is created. Successful people keep creating more ideas and generating more wealth.

The great thing about knowing how wealth is created is that there are no limits. Wealth is created through imagination and ideas. You can imagine anything, so the ability to create wealth is unlimited. If you do a job you can ask the universe to pay you one hundred dollars in return. You can just as easily ask it to pay one million dollars or ten million. There is no limit to the idea; the only limit is the one you place on it by your limiting beliefs. If you ask for the million dollars, you also need to develop action plans that have that goal in mind.

The four principles of creation must all be accomplished before the idea becomes reality. The first principle of Desire is used every day. Desiring things is fun. It takes only a little time and energy to think and imagine things you want. The second principle of Belief is not difficult but it is the reason most people fail to see their desires come true. The third principle of Exchange takes a commitment from you about what you are willing to give up in exchange for what you want. Exchange is something you do when you want something and have to work in order to get it. The fourth principle of Action takes the most effort. It requires you to make plans, get help, build strategy and work to make what you want a reality. You can be willing and able to do this, but without Belief it will all be a waste of time.

The second principle of Belief requires no investment, but it is the one that fails most often. The lack of belief is what stops you from creating a perfect life in a perfect world. Belief takes no time and no energy. It requires you to give up nothing, and it takes no effort or work. It only requires you to make a choice. You must choose to believe. It is the easiest principle to accomplish, but it's most often the reason you fail to have the type of life you desire. What would cause that?

Fear. You fear that you will fail and be disappointed. If you dare to believe, you are exposing yourself to the possibility of failure and disappointment. You would rather not get your hopes up. Instead of believing in yourself to accomplish great things, you choose to believe you will never accomplish anything and, therefore, you will not be disappointed.

When you think this way, you prove the principle works, but in a way to disappoint you. When you choose not to believe in yourself and choose to believe that you will not accomplish your goals and not become anything great, you are using the principles of creation to make your negative belief become reality. You set it into motion. Your belief and your actions make it real in your life.

You have the ability to create whatever you choose. If you want to create wealth for yourself, you have that choice and ability. If you want to choose failure for yourself, you also have that choice and ability. You are always creating your life. Because you may not be aware of it, you might be creating a life you do not like. When you doubt yourself, you are choosing to create a life of failure. When you believe the doubts, you set them into motion; you make plans and act in accordance with this belief until it is manifest fully in your life.

In this way you are always demonstrating the principles of creation within you to create whatever you choose. Jesus said that people perish because of their lack of knowledge. They fail when they do not understand the truth of how things work.

When you choose not to believe in your power to create, it is likely because you fear failures. When you fear failure, you have a belief that is out of balance with truth. You do not believe in your own divine connection to the Source. Otherwise you would believe in the possibility of creation. You also fear failure because you think it will bring disappointment and emotional hurt. This fear only exists when you think you are a person who can be hurt. The real you is the divine Source inside of you which cannot be hurt. Even in your failures , try to see how your thoughts and beliefs are at work producing the results of your own creation.

If you want to test the principles of creation, start with a small idea. Imagine a small success which you can believe in. Prove to yourself how this wonderful miracle works. When you see small victories, set bigger goals. When you achieve success, make a larger vision. Soon you will be making miracles every day and learning how to create peace, joy, happiness, health, and financial freedom.

People all over the world have been doing this since the beginning of time. Even though they may never have thought of it in terms of the Four Principles of Creation, it is the same thing. Most people who use this process may not think of it in terms of creation, but it is a principle of the universe which they know works. You can use this principle to create whatever you desire.

Emotions are teachers.

Learn their lessons well
and you will feel peace.

CHAPTER 7

Be Emotionally Aware

This chapter explains the importance of your emotions and how to remain aware of them without letting them control you. This is *Step Seven* of the **Ten Steps to Finding the Secret Inside**.

Ten Steps to Finding the Secret Inside

1. Understand your current perception
2. Heal your emotional pain
3. Look inside yourself
4. Choose new beliefs
5. Live in the present
6. Find creative power within you
7. **Be emotionally aware**
8. Align your personality
9. Embrace what "Is"
10. Transcend the illusion

Emotions are important because they allow you to feel whether you are happy, sad, in pain, angry, or at peace. Your emotional health determines the quality of your life.

Because emotions are important, it's worth the effort to understand how to use them to your benefit rather than allow them to hinder you. Emotions are your feedback system to inform you of whether or not your beliefs and thoughts are in balance with what you really want and with the Source inside you. Awareness of your emotions is an important aspect to maintaining peace and happiness.

Emotions are either positive or negative depending upon whether your thoughts are positive or negative. Your thoughts will be either positive or negative depending upon your beliefs.

If you believe, as I did, that there is a God in heaven, then when you pray to God because you hurt, you expect help to come. If you do not receive help you might feel abandoned, as I did. In this example, it is your belief in a certain type of god that leads to the pain.

Your belief in an external god causes you to expect that god to intervene in your life situations when you need help. When no help arrives, you feel abandoned, which leads to sorrow, anger, bitterness, and pain. More pain makes you want more help from God, and the cycle continues.

Emotions are a feedback system telling you when your thoughts and beliefs are in balance with the Source inside you and when they are not. The emotion of pain signifies your beliefs are not in balance. To correct the balance, change your thinking. If you ignore the emotional message and keep believing in the same way, the pain remains.

Experience the Emotion

Previously you learned how the Source separates into the parts of creation so that each part could be experienced. Through this process, all creation becomes more compassionate and evolves and improves. The separation is required for one part to experience the other part. Love cannot fully be realized until fear and hate and anger are also experienced. The contrast allows the difference to be experienced.

You will not know what fun is until you have experienced the opposite of fun. You cannot feel love until you have felt the lack of love. You cannot appreciate light unless you also have experienced darkness. You cannot appreciate sharing unless you also have experienced selfishness.

No part of creation is evil; all that exists has come from the Source and is therefore a part of the Source. Emotions of sadness, anger, resentment, and bitterness are no less valuable than love, kindness, and joy. Each is a part of the Source and each is intended to be experienced at least one time.

If you feel abandoned by God and feel anger, sorrow, or pain, take the opportunity to fully experience that emotion. Let it sink into the depths of your being and feel the pain. Feel what abandonment is; feel what anger is; and feel the sadness and loneliness.

Let Emotions Pass Through You

Now that you've found the miracle inside, you know you are part of the Source and no longer need to let pain remain with you. You are divine and can choose which emotions remain with you and which ones pass through you. You are a conscious thinking part of the Source, so you can choose to release the emotions you don't want.

The energy of the Source is housed in your body, but your body is not who you are. It is only used to allow you to occupy physical space to participate in this physical life. In the same way, your mind and thoughts aren't you either. They are tools for you to form ideas and beliefs, and to feel emotions. When you find the miracle inside, you gain control of directing your life, your mind, and your body toward the life you choose.

During your life you will experience many forms of emotions. By enduring negative feelings, you are better able to appreciate all the positive ones. Once you realize that you are part of the Source, you can choose to stay in the place where you experience only the incredibly good feelings, all the time.

For example: If you believed that there is a God as "somebody in heaven," then you feel abandoned when you don't receive help at the time you need it. You develop a feeling of abandonment and later anger, resentment, loss of faith, and bitterness toward God. For a short while it is fitting for you to experience and feel those emotions.

During the times you hurt, you think you are a person who needs to be taken care of; but you are not. You are not a lost child needing help from a father figure. You are part of the Source and the pain is there to indicate your imbalance with the truth inside. Part of the miracle is that the truth inside you is directing you toward it at all times. When you are in balance with the truth, then you feel good. When your beliefs and thoughts are not aligned with the truth, you feel pain. Because you are a part of the divine Source you cannot *be* hurt; you can only *feel* hurt when you believe a lie about who you are.

As you experience an emotion, remember why you are experiencing it. You feel emotions to point you toward the truth. If you pay attention to your emotions and take action to align your beliefs and thoughts with the truth, then you can expect joy all the time.

As soon as possible after experiencing the emotion of abandonment, anger, or sorrow, let go of that feeling. The emotions are not you; they are only an indicator of imbalance. If you fail to see yourself as separate from the emotion, you don't know how to let go. When this occurs, you attach the negative feeling of sadness, abandonment, or sorrow to yourself. You add it to who you think you are.

By doing so, you compound the false illusion about who you are. One negative experience may add to your illusion the idea that you are separated from your Source and not worthy of love. Your self-esteem will be lowered and you will find it more difficult to find your way back to love.

The world is full of opportunities to test your beliefs. All of your beliefs that are out of balance with the truth inside you will cause you to feel a negative emotion. This is your wonderful feedback system. Some people are supposed to be experiencing difficult times right now, just as you were supposed to have difficulties at some point. Those difficulties brought you to where you are now. They showed you the error in your thinking so that you could change it to be in balance with the truth and what you really want. Once you are in balance, your emotional feedback system never needs to send you negative emotions; you should experience total peace and bliss.

While living in this world full of opportunities to test your beliefs, make meditation a part of your life. Meditation is a good way to become aligned with the Source inside you; when you do that you feel happy. Eventually, your beliefs and thoughts become naturally aligned with the truth of who you are and you feel very good all the time. Until it becomes natural, make time throughout the day to meditate.

While in this restful state and with your mind under control, think about the truth that you are part of the eternal divine Source. You know deep inside that you are something more than a physical body and more than a mind with memories and thoughts. You know that you are a spectacular and divine being. You have a connection to your Source because you are a part of it. While meditating, teach the truth to your thinking mind.

Consciously tell yourself that you have existed since before the beginning of time. You have always been and always will be. Remember the Source created the illusion that your mind and body are separate from the Source. This illusion allowed you to experience many things that you could not otherwise have encountered. Now that you have undergone them, tell yourself that you wish to re-unite with your Source so that you no longer need to experience negative emotions.

Remind yourself that your job, your family and friends, the stuff you accumulate, and the problems you encounter are not important to your purpose. They are details of life that were necessary to bring you to the place you are now — a place of understanding the truth.

When you get sucked back into the illusion that life is about the details, you become stressed and begin to struggle. Those emotions are valuable because they are your automatic feedback system, showing that you are out of balance with the truth. Your goal should be to live in this world and not get sucked into believing the illusion. Walk the journey of this life and experience it, and know that you are part of the Source that created it all.

The Lesson of the Emotion

Emotions exist for two reasons; one is to experience fully all aspects of the creation; the second is to guide you to the truth. Belief forms thought; thoughts result in feelings. So, when you have feelings you don't like, trace them back to your beliefs. When you experience a negative emotion, feel it, gain the experience of the emotion so you never need to experience it again. Next, assess the belief which has brought about this negative emotion.

Following the previous example, when you feel abandoned by God, find the belief that elicits the feeling and adjust it. It is important to determine what belief is triggering the thought that causes the negative emotion. When you find the belief responsible for the pain, change the belief so you feel good about whatever is happening.

When you feel abandonment, anger, bitterness, pain, sorrow, or loneliness, think about what is happening. Those negative feelings do not correspond with the positive feelings you expect should be occurring. You think God should be responding, helping you, and intervening in your life situation so you can feel better. Recognize that your belief is not aligning with what is actually taking place. This is your signal, a signal to question and investigate further.

Your belief that God is separate from you causes feelings of abandonment when you get no response. The way to find peace in your life is to learn to balance the truth inside you with the reality of what is happening. Change your belief to one that is perfectly in balance with the reality of what is happening. The steps listed below are a guide to doing this.

Four Steps To Emotional Healing
1. Acknowledge the need for change.
2. What are your beliefs — how do you feel?
3. Consider better beliefs — how would you feel?
4. Adopt new beliefs — how will you feel?

If you feel abandoned by God, use the steps listed above. You hurt because you believed in a separate God who was supposed to come to your aid. Turn that around. Create a belief that God can never abandon you. Make it impossible for that idea to even exist. Choose to believe that your Source and you are one and the same. The Source is within you and you are within it. Choose to believe that the Source does not exist without you and you do not exist without it. The two are inseparable. Choose to form a new belief in which abandonment does not exist. If abandonment is not possible, you cannot hurt. There is no abandonment because there never was any separation. The Source never did separate from you; you and it are one.

When you create this new belief, you see that your prayers, your waiting, and your growing disappointment have been the result of your imbalanced beliefs. When you change your beliefs, you cannot feel abandonment.

The purpose of the emotion is to indicate your imbalanced beliefs. When you become discontent, you struggle, and you feel pain. When this occurs, apply the Four-Step Process to emotional healing. Experience the feeling. Ponder the feeling and ask yourself about the beliefs which could be causing the feeling. Turn that belief around and teach your mind the new enjoyable belief through meditation. Consider the following examples of how to put this into practice.

When your spouse or partner needs to change:

If you are in a relationship with a spouse or partner which is causing emotional strain, listen to what that emotion is telling you. It is not likely to be telling you to leave the relationship unless you are being abused. (In that case, leave). Otherwise, assume all things happen for a reason and that you are supposed to be right here, right now, experiencing this relationship. Find out what message you are supposed to learn so you can get back to living a completely happy and fulfilling life.

When you and your partner have a disagreement that causes stress, you tend to believe your partner needs to change. Or, you might even recognize your need to change, but believe you cannot change. When struggles come, recognize that negative emotions have come to tell you that you have a belief that is out of balance with the truth inside you. Change your belief in order to find peace.

When you believe your partner needs to change, you want the change so you can have peace. You believe your problems will be solved if your partner changes. When you have this belief and your partner does not change, you become angry and disappointed. You see your partner keeping you from having a happy, fulfilling, and peaceful life. How would you feel if you eliminated this belief or replaced it with an opposite one? Use the four-step process.

1. You already know you feel bad and don't want to feel this way

anymore. Acknowledge that change needs to occur.

2. What are your beliefs to experience this kind of pain? They might include:

+ My partner should change.
+ My partner hurts me on purpose.

How do you feel with those beliefs?

+ I feel hurt.
+ I feel angry.
+ I feel sorry for myself because no one else does.

3. Consider better beliefs that are in balance with what is happening.

+ My partner is supposed to be exactly the way they are. My partner is a part of the Source and is living their exact chosen life in order to experience the things they need to experience.

+ My partner's early environment caused them to be the way they are. All the emotional baggage my partner carries had to be custom-made through years of development. My partner had to be born into a specific family that provided specific pain necessary to help me become balanced and find peace now. My partner is part of the Source, living this specific human experience, partly for my benefit. My partner is supposed to be acting exactly this way, with all the anger, self-esteem issues, fears, and more.

✦ You might feel that your partner tries to hurt you on purpose because it looks that way. When it appears that way, do you feel hurt? If you feel hurt, you are out of balance with your Source. To get back into balance remember that you are the same as your Source. Do you see that you (the Source) cannot be hurt? It is because of the illusion that it looks as if you can be hurt. Outside the illusion you can see that your partner is another part of you, part of the same Source. When your partner appears to be the enemy, realize they are God in disguise to help you through this life journey. The hardest part of your journey is when you fail to believe that you and everyone else are part of the Source.

4. Adopt new beliefs.

How will you feel if you adopt these new beliefs?

✦ How does your perception of the relationship change when you believe that your partner is acting exactly as they are supposed to? Can you accept it and not try to change them? If you can, you will find peace in the relationship knowing that they are following their life plan exactly as they are supposed to.

✦ Your partner's entire life was custom-made to help you learn this lesson. Likewise, your life was custom-made to help your partner learn. Can you accept that they are not trying to hurt you? Rather, you are each trying to help each other; you are both part of the same Source. Your partner's actions can help you return to your Source, even if your partner is still stuck in the illusion.

Do you feel that by changing your beliefs to the above suggestions, you would be happier than if you keep your old beliefs? If so, then adopt the new beliefs that are in balance with the way things really are.

When you feel life should not be so hard:

Do you struggle and feel hopeless because life seems hard? Do you wish you could get ahead financially? Do you wish you had more time with your family, but don't know how to get it? Is it a struggle to get through every day?

If these struggles exist in your life, recognize that your emotions are indicating that you're out of balance with the truth inside you. Use the Four-Step Process to find the belief that is out of balance with the truth. It needs to be changed in order for you to have peace.

1. You already know you feel bad and don't want to feel this way anymore. Acknowledge that change needs to occur.

2. What are your beliefs to experience this kind of pain? They might include:

    ✦ Life is hard.
    ✦ Life is not supposed to be so hard.

    How do you feel with those beliefs?

    ✦ I feel tired.
    ✦ I feel hopeless.

✦ I feel sorry for myself because everything is so hard.

3. Consider better beliefs which are in balance with what is happening.

Consider that life really is not difficult. Consider that you only see it that way because you are stuck in the illusion of seeing yourself as separate from your Source. If you believe that you are the acting/thinking part of the Source, accept that life is not difficult; it only appears that way when you view yourself as separate from your Source.

4. Adopt new beliefs.

How will you feel if you adopt this new belief? If it brings peace, then adopt it as a new belief. If you believe it, you will start making changes in your life to bring about lasting happiness. You will become happy because you will find ways to create happiness.

When you feel "my boss/co-workers don't like me":

Work may be stressful because you believe your supervisor, your boss, or your co-workers don't like you; friction exists at work. You wish it could change, that they would leave, or that you could leave, but you feel trapped. Use the Four-Step Process for emotional healing.

1. You already know you feel bad and don't want to feel this way anymore. Acknowledge that change needs to occur.

2. What are your beliefs to experience this kind of pain? They might include:

+ People at work don't like me.
+ I need this job and cannot leave it.

How do you feel when you believe this?

+ I feel trapped.
+ I feel hurt.
+ I feel sorry for myself because others don't like me.

3. Consider better beliefs that are in balance with what is happening.

+ One belief to consider is that others actually do like you. You have no way to know for sure they don't like you, no matter what you are told, even if they say it to your face. Imagine that they are telling you a lie. Believe that there is a way they actually do like you; you just need to envision it.

+ Consider a new belief that you have value to the world in many ways and can get a job many places. Would you be happier if you felt free to leave your job any time you wanted, even if you chose to stay? Would changing your belief about feeling trapped help you feel happier? If so, adopt it.

4. Adopt new beliefs.

✦ How would you feel if you chose to believe that your co-workers do like you? Would you feel better? If so, adopt the new belief and meditate to teach it to your thinking mind. Tell yourself that they might not realize it, but they are part of the Source, as you are. They are part of you. They love you because they are you. Even though they are still stuck in the illusion, they agreed to live this way for a while for your benefit. Eventually, they too will benefit from what they are experiencing. In the end, you will all reunite with the Source.

✦ If this brings you peace, adopt it as a new belief. Act in this way every day by going to work, not because you have to, but because you want to. Believe that you can work anywhere you want and that you have freedom every day to choose where to work. You are a free person. You are the source of your own income. You create value by producing something for the world — either labor or ideas or services. Every day, know you have a choice about where you put your value to work.

I should be more successful:

Do you feel as if you are a failure or that you are not nearly as successful as you want to be? You might measure success with money, or a job title, or a business owned, or by the possessions and family you have or don't have. However you measure success, you believe you should have more of it. When you feel emotional stress, recognize that your beliefs and thoughts are not in balance with the truth. They need to be changed in order for you to have peace. Use the Four-Step Process.

1. You already know you feel bad and don't want to feel this way anymore. Acknowledge the need for change.

2. What are your beliefs to experience this kind of pain? They might include:

   ✦ I am not successful.
   ✦ I should be more successful.

   How do you feel when you believe this?

   ✦ I feel unworthy.
   ✦ I feel disappointed.
   ✦ I feel embarrassed.

3. Consider better beliefs that are in balance with what is happening.

   ✦ Consider that you are not supposed to be "successful" as you define it. You may be following the perfect plan for your life and this is exactly the way it is supposed to be. Can you find peace in that? If you can, then adopt it. If not, keep looking for a better belief.
   ✦ Consider a new belief, that you already are successful, but that you simply are not yet manifesting it. You might have all the knowledge and skills to be successful in the way you desire. Fear of failure or lack of confidence might be holding you back from pursuing your success in a way for it to become manifest. How do you feel about these new beliefs? Believe that you can change the situation by using the principles of creation.

4. Adopt new beliefs.

+ How would you feel if you changed your beliefs? If you want a family, a business, a promotion, more money, or something else, believe you can create it through the principles of creation. Believe in it, make a plan, and act on it until it arrives. If this new belief along with your new actions could make you happy, then embrace it.

My parents should have protected me:

You might have experienced situations of your childhood where you were abused, uncared for, neglected, or hurt in some way. Today you feel you are scarred from those events and will never be able to be free completely from the pain they still cause. You might have learned to cope with things the way they are and compensate in your life for the wounds of the past, but deep down you believe your parents could have and should have protected you better so you would not have been hurt.

The negative emotions you have indicate your beliefs and thoughts are out of balance with the truth inside you. Use the Four-Step Process to restore balance and peace.

1. You already know you feel bad and don't want to feel this way anymore. Acknowledge the need for change.

2. What are your beliefs to experience this kind of pain? They might include:

+ I am hurting because I was hurt as a child.

✦ My parents could have and should have protected me better.

How do those beliefs make you feel?

✦ I feel hurt.
✦ I feel angry at my parents.
✦ I feel sorry for myself because no one else does.

3. Consider better beliefs which are in balance with what is happening.

✦ I am no longer hurting because now I see myself as part of the Source of everything. I see that my belief was an illusion created so that I could feel emotions that otherwise could never have been experienced. I only thought I was hurting because I believed in the illusion that I am separate from my Source.

✦ My parents could not and should not have done anything differently than they did. They grew up with their own hurt and painful baggage and were stuck in the illusion of being separate from their Source when they raised me.

✦ My parents should not have acted any differently than they did because this is exactly what was planned for my life. This was required in order for me/Source to experience the depth of emotions that I experienced. This level of pain was required in order for me to look within myself and find the miracle inside bringing me back to become one with my Source.

4. Adopt new beliefs.

✦ How will you feel if you adopt any of these new beliefs? If you feel better, adopt them and meditate to plant these truths into your conscious mind.

My parents should have loved me more:

Do you wish your parents loved you more when you were growing up? Were your parents too busy for you? Did you want their attention, but rarely got it? Did you want their approval, but found you were never good enough no matter how hard you tried? Did your parents put you up for adoption?

As a child you tried to get approval and tried to get love, but no matter how hard you tried, you could not. As an adult you might not realize the link to your childhood; today you still fight to be loved and accepted, and to be good enough, to be worthy of being loved. The pain today is the same as your pain as a child. Today there are different circumstances and different people involved in your life, but the painful emotions are the same familiar ones that you have struggled with all your life. The emotions are sending you a message that you hold a belief that is out of balance with the truth inside you. Use the Four-Step Process to restore balance and peace to your life.

1. You already know you feel bad and don't want to feel this way anymore. Acknowledge the need for change.

2. What are the beliefs you hold for you to experience this kind of pain? They might include:

    ✦ My parents did not love me.
    ✦ My parents should have loved me.

+ I am not worthy of being loved.
+ I am not good enough.

How do you feel about these beliefs?

+ I feel unworthy and rejected.
+ I feel sorry for myself because no one else is doing it for me.
+ I feel angry at those who won't love me as I want.

3. Consider better beliefs aligned with what is happening.

+ Consider that your parents could not show you more love because they did not know how. They have similar hurts from their childhoods, and they might not know how to love you in the way you desire.

+ Consider that your parents do love you, but based on your own biased perception of reality, you cannot see it.

+ Consider that your parents are not supposed to love you Might there be a grand plan, formed long before you were born (while you and your parents were spiritual beings united with the Source) where you all agreed to live these lives in the manner you experienced as the only way for you to encounter such pain? In reality you and your parents are part of the same Source. You and your parents are connected as one. You agreed to live in the illusion and your parents agreed to live in the same illusion, allowing you and them to experience this pain. The pain might have been the only thing big enough to push you toward looking within yourself to find the miracle of the truth inside. Now that you know the truth about who you are, you have the choice to step out of the illusion and see that in reality you cannot be hurt. You created the entire experience of being separate in order for you to go through something that could never have been encountered without the illusion.

4. Adopt new beliefs.

    How would you feel if you adopted new beliefs?

    + Would you be happy if you choose to believe your parents actually do love you?

    + Would you by happy if you choose to believe your parents could not love you because they didn't know how?

    + Would you be happy if you choose to believe your parents are not supposed to love you in order to fulfill your own pre-designed plan for your life?

    If these beliefs would make you happy, adopt them as your own. Your emotions will tell you whether or not you are in balance by how they make you feel.

A desire is in you
to know who you are
to find your home.

Thoughts are the roads.
Some lead away;
others bring you home.

CHAPTER 8

Align Your Personality

This chapter will help align your personality with your new beliefs. The last chapter focused on changing your thinking and beliefs. This chapter focuses on changing your behavior and actions. This is *Step Eight* of the **Ten Steps to Finding the Secret Inside.**

Ten Steps to Finding the Secret Inside

1. Understand your current perception
2. Heal your emotional pain
3. Look inside yourself
4. Change your beliefs
5. Live in the present
6. Find creative power within you
7. Be emotionally aware
8. *Align your personality*

9.   Embrace what "Is"
10.   Transcend the illusion

You constructed your personality when you were a child. You have the choice to keep the one you created or change it now that you are older and wiser. Most people keep the one they created because they don't understand how to change it. That personality causes you to behave in ways that might not align with what you really want. Confusion and suffering are the result.

Your personality has a purpose. It is used to interact with the world around you. It provides a way for you to communicate with the world and for the world to communicate with you. You create things in your mind and project them to the world through your personality by what you think, say, and do. The world sends you feedback and you feel it through your emotions.

Your personality sends out energy that is either positive or negative. When your personality is aligned with your Source, your thoughts, words, and actions produce positive energy that promotes love in the world. The love you project to the world reflects right back to you. When you send out love, you feel love.

When your personality is not in balance with the Source inside, you project negative energy to the world. You may not realize you are projecting negative energy until later when it reflects back to you and you feel disappointment or pain.

Being in balance

If you welcome joy and peace into your life, you are in balance. If you are not experiencing joy and peace, it is because your beliefs, thoughts and actions are out of balance with what you want.

Being in balance means you align your personality and actions with the knowledge of who you are and train your personality to project love. If you want love, you are in balance when you produce love and project it to all those around you. If you want to feel happy, you are in balance when you project a positive personality to all those around you.

If you wish to be wealthy, you are in balance when you project the ideas and attitude of abundance to all those around you, rather than project the idea that money and possessions are limited and scarce. If you want freedom, you are in balance as long as you project the idea of freedom to all those around you.

Balance starts with knowing who you are. Balance is maintained by focusing on what is important. What is important is how you *deal* with the details of life, not the details themselves. It is not important if you get the job you desire or if you get fired from the job you have. What is important is whether or not you believe in your ability to influence the details of your life. It is important how you react when the details unfold in a way you do not like. And it is important how you treat those around you. "Do unto others as you would have them do unto you."

When people attempt to do you wrong, it's not important that they are doing you wrong and it's also not important for you to be "right" in the situation. Your response is what matters, how you think, act, and feel about it. It is important to remember that you are a part of your Source that cannot be hurt and that the people attempting to hurt you are part of the same Source as you, even though they might not know it. It's also important to realize that in the beginning when you were united with the Source, you planned to live your life for a while without remembering who you are, but only for a while.

Others may act against you because they do not know that you are both part of the same Source. They don't understand that they are only projecting actions to hurt themselves. The way to have genuine compassion for others is to realize that they are not hurting you; they are projecting pain onto themselves.

The detail of what others do to you is not important, nor is the fact that they are doing it intentionally to hurt you. It is only important how you respond. No matter what they project, send only love to them and to everyone around you, because what you give out is what you will feel. As long as you do this you will feel only the love you are projecting. People lost in their illusion of being separate will feel the pain of the attitudes they are projecting; this is how they are hurting themselves. If you want to feel love, there is one thing you must do, always: project love to everyone around you.

Being out of balance

When you recognize that you are projecting things different from what you want, decide to change what you are projecting. This means you need to change your personality — the way you think and act toward others. To do this, remember that you are not your personality. The personality is a package of ideas, beliefs, and memories which you made when you were a child. That package needs to change.

When you were feeling bad, you projected an attitude which you are now reaping. How you feel about the world is a reflection of what you project to it. If you do not like something in your world, you can change it by changing something in yourself. You must change the part of your personality responsible for sending out negative energy.

Defining what must change

When your life is joyful and you are satisfied with every aspect of it, there is no reason to change. If you experience anything less than total satisfaction and happiness, find the part of your personality responsible for sending out the negative energy and change it.

Evaluate what makes you happy. The natural tendency is to believe your happiness is dependent upon things outside yourself. It is easy to be unhappy with your neighbor who dumps garbage onto your property. It is easy to be unhappy with the co-worker who speaks badly about you. It is easy to be unhappy with a boss who does not like you.

You might feel anger with terrorists or even the government for sending your country to war. You might feel anger because you were the victim of robbery. You might hurt because your family rejects you. You might feel pain because you were molested or abused.

There are millions of examples of things outside yourself that seem valid reasons to feel hurt, sad, or angry. When you live in the illusion that you are separate from your Source, all these reasons appear legitimate.

Legitimate or not, if you allow your happiness to be influenced by anything outside yourself, you will never find peace. Your happiness cannot depend on the people around you or depend upon any life circumstance. Your happiness must be based on knowing you are a part of your Source.

When life brings you pain, examine your beliefs and find the one that needs to change. Only a belief which is out of balance with truth will allow you to feel pain. You may not be able to control the outside circumstances in your life, but you surely can control your feelings about them; you can have peace within every circumstance. Outside circumstances will continue to be what they are, but your beliefs will determine how you feel about them.

After you develop new beliefs, train yourself to think and act in alignment with them. Since birth, you have developed habits of thinking and acting certain ways. Those behaviors may have been based on beliefs that were out of balance with the truth. Some of those thought patterns and behaviors projected negative energy to the world through your personality. Those are what need to change. When you align your personality to interact with the world in a manner that is aligned with the perfection of your Source, then you create a perfect life for yourself.

Remember, your old beliefs resulted in your old behaviors, which resulted in struggle and pain. You want new outcomes in your life which are opposite of struggle and pain. In order to create that, learn to choose opposite beliefs, which will result in positive feelings. Now, to be sure that desire becomes manifest completely, choose new behaviors which are also opposite of your old ego-centered behaviors.

Previous examples conveyed how to find beliefs that were out of balance with the truth inside you. You were shown examples of what those out-of-balance beliefs might be and you were provided with some suggestions for changing those beliefs. Now, consider those same examples to see how your behavior must also change to align with your new beliefs.

When your spouse or partner needs to change:

Old behaviors:

+ I tried to change my partner by pointing out their faults.
+ I needed to prove myself right; I argued.
+ I needed to defend my position; I degraded my partner.
+ I tried to get appreciation by asking for it and pointing out my own good deeds.

<u>Replace Old Behavior With These New Behaviors</u>

+ I tried to change my partner.　　➡ Change myself.
+ I needed to prove myself right.　➡ Find my partner right.
+ I needed to defend my position.　➡ Defend my partner.
+ I tried to get appreciation.　　　➡ Appreciate my partner.

How to practice new behaviors:

Change yourself

Rather than feel the need to change your partner, change yourself. The new belief indicates that your partner is supposed to be the way they are. They grew up in the specific environment that made them that way. You and your partner are both part of the Source and agreed to come to earth to live these lives. You both chose behaviors designed to bring about the changes desired in each other. The timing for your partner to change is not up to you. Focus your attention on changing you.

Rather than waste time looking at your partner's faults, take that time to be aware of your own emotions and allow them to guide you to build new beliefs. Then consider your thoughts and behaviors and determine if your thoughts and behaviors are aligned with these new beliefs. Take inventory of what behaviors you want to change and work at changing them until they become habit.

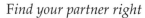

Find your partner right

In the past you felt the need to be right and prove yourself right, which led to arguments. Assuming you went through the process to form new beliefs about who you are, you no longer need to prove yourself right. You might also now believe that your partner comes from the same divine Source as yourself.

Spend time to find the good things in your partner and state them. Your partner grew up with hurts, as most people did. They may or may not understand that they are a part of the divine Source. By praising the goodness you see in them, you plant positive seeds that will come back to you, and help move them toward finding their own truth.

Defend your partner

Rather than defending yourself at the expense of your partner, look for ways to defend them. They might feel vulnerable and hurt, as most people do. Your partner might still believe in the illusion that they are separate from their Source. As humbly as you can, defend them by never initiating arguments. Forego some of your opportunities so they can have them. Defend them by allowing them to believe they are right, even when you feel otherwise. Allow them to have the last word in a disagreement if that makes them feel better.

Appreciate your partner

Rather than look for your own appreciation, encourage your partner. With your new belief that you are both connected to your Source, you know that when you build them up, you are also building up yourself. Praise the good in them and help them succeed. When you promote your partner, you reap the rewards of peace, love, success, and happiness for yourself.

When you feel life should not be so hard:

Work is stressful. You have financial burdens, limited time, family obligations, and growing responsibilities. You believe life is hard.

Old behaviors:
+ I worked hard and long.
+ I didn't make time to eat healthy foods, sleep enough, or exercise sufficiently.
+ I didn't have time to help others.

Replace Old Behavior With These New Behaviors
+ I worked too much.   ⇒ Work with less effort.
+ I took too little time to eat, ⇒ Make time for these.
  sleep, and exercise.
+ I took no time to help others. ⇒ Make time to help others.

How to practice new behaviors:

Work with less effort

The effort required to complete tasks is proportionate to the belief you have about how difficult it should be. When you choose to believe that things are easy and that you can accomplish great things, you no longer need to exert so much time and effort. Practice the Four Principles of Creation to make work become easier and require less time.

Make time to eat, sleep, and exercise

Using the principles of creation, you attract more money into your life. Use that money to buy yourself more time. Do this by creating jobs for others with the money you've attracted into your life. Many people want to earn money by doing your yard work, household chores, washing your cars, and anything else that takes your time.

By giving jobs to others, you help yourself as well. You give out money, which also strengthens the belief that money is not important to you and that you can always make more as often as needed.

Give as much away as possible by creating jobs for others. This buys you time to sleep more, eat better, and exercise. These new behaviors build habits that change your old belief that life is hard. As you do, you come to see the truth that life is not hard at all. Life is easy, fun, enjoyable, and pleasant. You soon find that your old belief was an elaborate illusion that kept you from having a wonderful life.

Make time to help others

The reason you don't help others is because you believe time and money are limited and that you cannot even meet your own needs. When you change this belief and practice attracting money into your life, you can buy more time.

Practice helping others to prove that you have available free time to give away. When you give it away with the belief that you will receive more free time, it will come. Continue to build wealth by creating jobs for others, giving away money, and giving away your free time. It will all come back to you. This is sometimes referred to as the "law of attraction."

When you feel "my boss/co-workers don't like me":

Old Behaviors:

✦ I work extra hard to get others to like me.

✦ I dislike those who don't like me.

Replace Old Behavior With These new Behaviors

✦ I work hard to be liked. ➡ Love myself.

✦ I dislike others. ➡ Give love to all.

How to practice new behaviors:

Love yourself

When you feel insecure because you have not found your identity, you try hard to be liked by others. You place your happiness and sense of worth in other's hands. Once you feel the pain associated with that belief, you can decide to believe you are the Source of all love.

With the new belief, you no longer need the affection and love of others in order to feel happy. Nothing is wrong with the affection of others, but something is wrong with the feeling that you *need* it to be happy.

Practice feeling love for yourself and others. During meditation, focus on this love. By strengthening this love, you no longer need the love of others in order to be happy. Stop wasting time being concerned whether or not others like you; instead, spend time loving yourself.

Give love to all those around you

Your old behaviors were based on your need to receive love

from others. With knowledge that you are the Source of love, you no longer *need* to receive it from others and you can spend time giving it away.

Giving love to those who might not like you is a behavior opposite to that of your old ego-based personality. By behaving in this way, you prove that you don't need love from others because you have love for yourself, with extra to give away. When you give it away, you receive it back into your life in many ways.

It was difficult to like others who disliked you when you believed they were separate from you. Now that you believe that you all originate from the same Source, it is easier to love them. Also, you now realize they might be stuck in the illusion and suffering their own pain. Your love may help them through that pain. Eventually, their release from the pain will bring more peace to you.

I should be more successful:

Old behaviors:
+ I do not pursue my passion.
+ I choose the security of working for others.
+ I spend more time thinking about saving money than about ways to create wealth.
+ I save money by doing things myself rather than providing jobs for others.

Replace Old Behavior With These New Behaviors
+ I don't pursue ideas.   → Start pursuing my passion.
+ I work a secure job.   → Start a side business.
+ I always think about saving.   → Imagine creating wealth.
+ I never hire help.   → Provide jobs for others.

How to practice new behaviors:

Start pursuing your passion

The most successful and happy people are those who do what they love to do. Imagine you are immensely wealthy and never need to work again. In this situation, how would you spend your time? Find something you want to do that also creates value to the world. This is the thing you should consider doing with the rest of your life, starting now.

Once you know what you want to do, imagine all the ways to bring it about. Even if it seems impossible, force yourself to imagine what must happen in your life to make it possible. Then practice the principles of creation to set it into motion.

Each day meditate on the ideas of your imagination. Make a plan of all the things that must come about in order for your ideas to become reality. There might be people you need to meet, financing that must be in place, business plans made, and more. Every day begin chipping away at the details of what must be done to achieve your dream. If you use the principles of creation and work every day to move toward your goal, you become the success you always dreamed of being. It will be of value to the world and it will be something you don't do just for money, it will be something you love to do.

Start a side business

Even if you have chosen the security of working for others rather than pursuing your own passion, you can begin changing, one step at a time. If your passion involves starting your own business, the first steps may be to make a business plan and get financing in place. It might be possible to start a business during your free time while you keep your income-making job.

Imagine creating wealth; stop thinking about saving

Those who know how to create wealth think the opposite way from those who do not know how to create wealth. Those who don't create wealth think often about how much everything costs and about ways to spend less and save more. This reinforces the belief that money is limited and scarce. They are likely to: clip coupons, spend hours traveling to multiple stores to save a few dollars on groceries, park blocks away from their destination to save parking fees, or spend hours or days looking for sales to save a hundred dollars on clothing. Nothing is wrong with doing those things. It simply supports the false idea that money is scarce. That type of thinking will never lead to the accumulation of wealth; it always leads to "never having enough money for what you want."

To change this behavior, first change your beliefs about the availability of money. With the time that you used to spend trying to save money, meditate and ask how to create money in ways that are meaningful to the world and enjoyable to you. You will be able to imagine ways to do things you love that bring value to others and which create many times more money than you could have saved through your previous frugal efforts. Change from acting frugal to acting out of abundance by sharing your money with others.

Create jobs for others; don't do it all yourself

If you believe money is scarce you tend not to hire others to work for you. You might mow your own lawn, do all your own house cleaning and yard work, work on your car, make house repairs, and more. This takes time when you could be doing more enjoyable things. Nothing is wrong with doing those things if you enjoy doing them. But, if you are only doing them because you "have no money," that is out of balance with the truth of abundance.

When you understand the principles of creation and how to use them, you know you can create wealth with your thoughts. It takes only a small amount of time to relax, think, and meditate to form ideas. When you are too busy doing chores, you will not have time to think about how to create wealth. If you want this to change, alter your behavior to make more time for yourself by hiring people to help you.

If you fail to believe you can create your own wealth, you will be reluctant to hire people to help you. This demonstrates the weakness of your belief, which will cause you to remain in a situation where money is always scarce. But, if you believe in your ability to create abundance, hire others to assist you. Providing jobs for others is what planting seed is to the farmer. Give to others and it will come back to you a hundred or thousand times.

By hiring others, you have more time to create and implement your wealth-making ideas. Use all four principles of creation and pursue them until your dreams become reality.

My parents should have protected me:

Old behaviors:
+ I keep trying to get my parents' approval/love.
+ I avoid my parents.
+ I strive to raise my children better.

<u>Replace Old Behavior</u> <u>With These New Behaviors</u>

✦ I still want approval/love.	↝ Love myself.
✦ I avoid my parents.	↝ Stop avoiding; just be!
✦ I swear I'll do better with my children.	↝ Raise my children with with love.

How to practice new behaviors:

Love yourself — rather than seek love from parents

Love from others can never satisfy your inner need to be loved, no matter how wonderful it is. Because the Source inside causes you to feel that something is missing in your life, search until you find the miracle inside yourself. You have always been divine, but you choose to forget for a while. During that time, your inner Source craves to be found so that it can produce the love that will satisfy forever. Nothing outside you will stop that craving.

Use meditation to become reunited with the Source inside you. By loving the Source that made you, you love yourself. When you find the Source, you do not need love from others in order to be happy. After finding this love, share it with those around you. Smile at strangers. Be kind to those you know, even to those who were hard to like in the past — even to the parents you felt did not love you.

Share your love because you are the Source of love and because both you and your parents come from the same Source. One day they too will know who they are. By giving your love away, you plant seeds that will grow and be reflected back into your own life.

Stop avoiding parents

When you avoid your parents because of all your past hurts, your actions reinforce your own pain. Stop avoiding your parents and you will weaken the pain and its hold on your life. You learn to heal your personality and find the Source inside you. When you do this, you no longer need to avoid anyone.

The more you project love to your parents, without conditions, the more you will be free. If you give love expecting to be loved back, you are using the wrong motives. You are the Source of all love. The Source of love does not give love expecting or needing it to be returned. The Source gives out love because it produces more than it needs. Give love to your parents, not because they deserve it, but because you are the Source of love. You have awakened to who you are; some day at the right time, they will too.

Raise your own children with love

You might swear to raise your children better than the way your parents raised you. You believe you can give your children more love. When you think this way, you are strengthening the belief that you were not loved, which keeps you feeling hurt. Don't compare your parents to yourself. If you do, you will end up being like them whether you want to or not, because you set into motion the principles of creation.

Remember, the principles of creation are less about what you say and more about what you concentrate on. If you spend time concentrating on how bad your parents were and how you want to be better, most of your thought energy is focused on the mental picture of how bad your parents were. This brings about the creation of these very behaviors in you. You will become just like them, even if you see yourself differently. Your own children will grow up and might view *you* in a similar manner.

To change this, change your belief and then your behavior. Heal yourself; then create new beliefs and actions that are in balance with the truth inside you. Give love to your children because you produce love inside yourself, not because you compete with your parents.

What you see

may not be what is.

What is

may not be what you see.

CHAPTER 9

Embrace What "Is"

This chapter shows how to love life the way it "is." This is **Step Nine** in the **Ten Steps to Finding the Secret Inside**.

Ten Steps to Finding the Secret Inside

1. Understand your current perception
2. Heal your emotional pain
3. Look inside yourself
4. Choose new beliefs
5. Live in the present
6. Find creative power within you
7. Be emotionally aware
8. Align your personality
9. ***Embrace what "Is"***
10. Transcend the illusion

The universe is full of events in which you participate and which you observe. Some of those events evoke good feelings and others evoke bad feelings. Welcome to the zone where you control everything —The Inside Zone. Here you do not need a teacher and you do not need a PhD to understand your own happiness. Here you are your own teacher; you already have the answer, you just need to find it inside you. This chapter looks at the way you perceive the events of the world around you, particularly how those events make you feel, and how to find happiness in everything that happens in your life.

You will learn how to find meaning, purpose, and peace with those things that currently bring struggle and pain. You will find power within you to immediately change the way you feel about those events and ultimately to change those events into something good and perfect.

What You See

Joy

You might find joy in watching small children at play. If you have children, you find joy when they give you their love and affection, their smiles, hugs, and kind words. You find joy in seeing them grow, mature, and become adults who still love you. Joy is also found in seeing new life come into this world. You might find it in the spring flowers that blossom from the garden you planted, or in the birth of your child, your grandchild, or children of friends. New life arrives full of innocence, full of love, neutral in experience, with no negativity or past baggage.

You might find happiness in seeing the people you love grow, accomplish their dreams, and find joy in their own lives. You might feel happy when you or a loved one gets good grades after working hard, graduates, gets a promotion, or wins a sporting event. Joy is found in romance, relationships, weddings, birthdays, and celebrations. Over time families grow up and often become separated. Then joy is found in reunions and catching up with each other's lives.

These events and others bring you happiness, joy, purpose and reason to enjoy life. These are the events that you wish would dominate your life all the time. Unfortunately, there are other events that bring unhappiness, disappointment, struggle and pain.

Struggles

You see disease in your own life in different forms. In the workplace, in schools, and at home you experience the cycles of the flu, colds, sore throats, and coughing. The disruption to your life and your family is mild yet real. You don't consider that this sickness has any reason or purpose for existing or entering into your life. Sickness is useless, a waste of time, yet a part of normal life. You take the bad with the good.

On a larger scale you see disease take away joy from friends, family, and others nearby. Things such as cancer, stroke, autism, and AIDS cause people you know to lose joy, lose vitality or lose life. What possibly can be the purpose and reason for this? These circumstances are painful, difficult, and there is no explanation for them. Life contains both the good and the bad, and you feel you cannot control any of it.

You see relationships crumble and feel pain yourself when you are hurt by those you love. You question why and strive to understand. You want to protect yourself and want to know why

SECRETS OF THE MIRACLE INSIDE

the people you love hurt you. Sometimes, with great effort, you might use compromise to keep your relationships in tact. Or, you might experience separation from friends, family, or your partner. These events bring pain, but isn't that a part of life?

In the world you see hunger, poverty, crime, terrorism, death, and war. These are all large-scale events outside your control and influence. Yet they affect you. You cannot find reason for these things to exist, yet here they are. You acknowledge that they appear to be a part of life; you deal with them the best way you can.

You or someone you know might have their freedom taken away. People are manipulated, controlled, and forced to do what they do not want to do. Children are abused and their lives ruined.

On a smaller scale you struggle with difficulties every day. You wake up late so you don't have time to get coffee. What a struggle the day will be; it starts bad and will only get worse. At work people pressure you to get more done, meet deadlines, coordinate schedules, events, and more.

Mixed events — Good and Bad

The world is full of both types of events; those that make you feel good, those that make you feel bad, and some are a mixture of both.

At work you find people you enjoy, you build friendships, you take pride in accomplishment, and through learning and experience you grow and improve. Those are the good things. But along the way you also might experience strife, confrontation, anger, hurt, jealousy, or consequences of people who resist and fight against you.

You might enjoy good health; you might have pain. Life might be a mix, some good, and some bad. You might want to lose weight. You pursue that desire by implementing diet and exercise programs. You might swim, run, work out at the gym, or do yoga. These are fun and fulfilling. But along the journey of life you might experience things about your body's health that make you feel bad. Sports get harder to do the older you get. Your weight increases and it is more difficult to lose. Your skin wrinkles, your hair turns grey or falls out, and you fear you won't ever look as good as you once did.

You might develop health problems, such as sleep apnea, high cholesterol, diabetes, or others ailments which degrade the quality of your life in some manner. Why do these things exist? You may never understand a reason for them or see a purpose. You know they cause you to feel bad and you want to be happy and full of joy. Yet events in the world and in your own life cause disappointment, struggle, and pain.

Attempting to change reality/the world

You believe there are two types of events in the world: those that make you feel good and those that make you feel bad. You have always seen the world that way and you accept it. However, you do not like the events that make you feel bad. Some of those events are not in your control; you cannot do anything to change them. You try to change other events so they no longer make you feel bad. Since you want to feel good more often and want to feel bad less often, you attempt to eliminate or at least reduce those events, actions, people, or behaviors that bring you the bad feelings, struggles, or pain.

You do this by:

+ Actively opposing by fighting what you do not want.
+ Resisting by avoidance.
+ Attempting to change what you do not like.

You might fight against the terrorist actions by supporting the troops who go to war. Or, if you disagree with the war you might oppose it by joining an anti-war demonstration. You might fight for: the war on drugs, the war against crime, Mothers against Drunk Drivers, free speech, freedom of religion, the war against cancer or AIDS.

You resist those things which make you feel bad or bring pain. You avoid being near those people who have hurt you. You might refrain from going to family or school reunions because of painful memories. You might stay away from situations where you could fail because you do not want to experience the memory of past failures and pain.

You might attempt to change your life to eliminate the things that make you feel bad and increase the things that make you feel good. You might attempt to change people at work to act in the manner you need in order to feel good. You might attempt to change the behavior of your children, your siblings, your parents, or your friends, in order for you to feel good. You might attempt to change your body through exercise, diet, pills, or medicine intended to give you a quick fix and make you feel good.

You do not accept the world the way you see it. You want to change it because you believe that is the way to make you feel good more often and feel bad less often. The reality is, both types of events exist in the world — the ones that make you feel good and the ones that make you feel bad. Both are here for good reason;

both have purpose; both are part of a plan for your life which is perfect in every way. You can learn to feel good about all of it — all the time.

The purpose of the events in your life

When your life was conceived in the mind of the Source that created all things, *you* were the purpose. The events around your life and in your life were *not* the primary purpose for creation. *You* were the purpose of creation and the events in your life only bring support to your development. "You" refers to the real *you* that is between the spaces of your thoughts, the inner-self.

All the events in your life reflect a picture of that inner self so that you see what you look like. When you see things in the world that make you feel good, you are experiencing a part of you that is in balance with what you want and with your purpose. When you witness events that cause you to feel bad you are seeing a reflection of your inner self that is not aligned with what you want.

The world is created to act as a mirror to show you your inner self. The events of the world reflect *you* to your conscious mind. When you see events that you do not like, you perceive the problem to be the events themselves. But the events need not be your focus. The events are only important because they are *your* mirror reflecting what *you* believe and think. When you attempt to change the events, or people, or situation around you, it is because you assume that they are the problem and that they can be changed.

Your reflection in the mirror

The world is the mirror and the events in your life are only reflections of what you think and believe. The mirror is not broken; the reflection is accurate and true. When you attempt to change the circumstances and events that you do not like, it is like trying to fix a perfect mirror which is reflecting an authentic picture of reality. The mirror is showing the reality of what you are at that moment in time. The mirror reflects exactly what you produce inside yourself. When you see events that cause you pain, the only reason you experience pain is because of the way you inaccurately perceive that event. The world reflects the inaccuracy to you by letting you see the event as a *bad* situation rather than as a *good* one.

When you experience events in life that make you feel good, it is because you have a belief that allows you to accept that event as it "is," and to embrace that event with love. You think of it in a positive way and you produce positive emotion. This process of thinking, believing, and producing positive emotions, is the principle of creation that sets into motion the positive energy which is sent from you to the world around you. Accordingly, that energy must be balanced by returning to you the same positive energy by making you feel good inside.

For example: When you believe that children are born innocent, with the ability to love, be funny, be entertaining, and give love, you set into motion the energy for this creation to become manifest in you. You see children playing in a park and you accept what you see. Even if the children are not perfect, you see them as enjoyable, non-threatening, and fun to be around. You hold this belief and accept what you see and emanate the emotion of pleasure. You experience joy and pleasant emotions associated with this event. You experience this good feeling, not because the event is inherently good, but because of the energy you initiated about that event through your own beliefs, thoughts and emotions.

Other events make you feel bad because you and others think they are bad and don't accept them as "is." You fight against them, avoid them, or try to change them. By the mere act of giving your negative thoughts and attention to those events, you cause them to exist and to expand. Those events only exist in the world because you and others give your attention to them. You believe these events are bad and you generate negative thoughts and emotions about them, setting into motion the creation and expansion of the exact thing which you oppose.

For example: War of any kind is brought on when people become aware of the issues and hold negative perception in their mind. By believing a false or negative thought about the enemy, negative emotions are formed and they set into motion the creation of the exact thing they oppose. They generate negative energy which causes conflict to expand. More people become enraged and want to fight "the enemy." As more and more people get on board with the struggle and more people hold negative beliefs and negative thoughts, the conflict grows.

Your Source created every detail of your life and all the events surrounding your life to bring about a specific positive result for you. Even those things that appear as negative are really positive; you just may not yet understand why. If you do not see it as a positive, find another way to look at it. You can be sure it is a good thing because otherwise you would not be experiencing it. That idea can be accepted if you choose to believe that all things are part of a divine plan and are in your best interest.

Accepting the way it "is"

The world is always the way it should be. When you accept that idea, there can be no hardship or pain. When you embrace the way the world is, there are no difficult decisions to make. There is no more feeling bad about anything. There is no wishing things were different because you know, for this moment, it is supposed to be exactly as it is. Right now you can have total peace.

All the details of your life are exactly the way they are because it is the plan for this very moment. Your family, your job, your friends, your enemies, your living condition, your financial situation, your level of happiness or lack of it, your pain, your struggle, and the fact you are reading this book now are all things that are exactly as they are supposed to be. They are that way because you influenced them to be that way through your own thoughts and beliefs. The circumstances in your life reflect your beliefs which set into creation all the details of your life.

When you see that events in the world happen *for* you rather than *to* you, you find joy in it all. Events you perceive as "bad," the ones that make you feel bad, are the reflection in the mirror to show you something inside. If you want to change the bad feeling you must change the thing inside you that causes the bad feeling, about the reflected event.

Things that happen to you are not the problem. The problem is the thought you have about what is happening. The things occurring are neutral; you have the choice to see them as either positive or negative. You will feel better by choosing to see everything as positive. The amazing thing is that right now you get to choose the future details of your life.

You will be happiest when you stop fighting against the way

the world is and accept what "is." By accepting reality, you accept that crime happens, wars kill, disease takes life, people hurt others, and hunger and poverty exist. Accepting these things as reality does not mean you like them. It just means you recognize them as reality, as much as you recognize love, joy, celebrations, and all the happy events of your life as reality. You do not place judgment on either type of event.

All events are placed in this world or placed in your life for specific reasons, which you might not yet understand. Believe they all have good reasons to exist. Accept all events equally because the world is a mirror reflecting what is inside you. There is no need to judge the mirror because the mirror is doing its job perfectly. The same is true with the specific events of the world; they are doing a job to teach you about yourself. Don't focus on the events until you have first corrected the issue inside you that causes you to see these events as a struggle.

In order to accept the world the way it is, you might need to define new beliefs that you have about the events causing you difficulty. Refer to previous chapters on how to accomplish that. When you form beliefs that allow you to see the divine purpose in all things and accept the world as it is without judgment, then you can initiate action at will to promote positive change for any of those events.

How to change events in your life
(now that you've accepted what "is")

The only way to change anything is by doing it inside you. When you focused on an event as an external problem it was because you did not understand that the world was a mirror reflecting something in you that needed to change. In that state, (of focusing on the "problem" event), if you tried to change the external event you would be using the principles of creation to make the problem expand and get worse, causing more struggles in your life.

The only way to make change is to first understand that events are connected as part of the Source and part of you. Meditate on the things that bother you and ask your Source to show you why they exist.

Consider that all events in life are part of a divine plan that you created before you were born into this world. If you are part of the Source that created everything, you have existed in some form since before the beginning of time. You have been a part of the consciousness that set into motion the creation of the universe and your own life. The events of your life were planned by you to bring about the desired experiences, most importantly the realization of who you are and how to find your way back to complete peace, joy, happiness, and power.

See that the events of the world are not nearly as important as the perceptions you have about them. Misfortune, hunger, poverty, disease, and death bring sadness and bad feelings when you believe these things are out of anybody's control and when you believe people are hurting. If you believe that everyone gets to plan out their life and that they do so in order to bring about the exact life experience they desire, then it is easier to accept what you see happening in the world around you.

When you see babies die from abuse or malnutrition, it hurts if you believe this is unfair and that these babies lost the opportunity to live their lives. However, if you believe that people get to live many lives, it is easier to accept that people sometimes choose to live the prospering life of a wealthy and healthy person and other times choose to live the life of a starving baby dying of malnutrition.

The events are simply events of creation here to manifest the perfect plan which you may not yet understand. But when you meditate and ask for revelation, you will be given answers to help you understand. Eventually you will come to see that the world really is only perfect. There is no misfortune; there is no evil and pain unless you choose to make it that way for yourself.

When you are able to see the world as a perfect place, you may still wish to influence and change some things that you see. For example, as you learn no longer to feel pain for starving children, you may have compassion for them and take action to help them, feed them, adopt them, or raise money to assist them.

This is an entirely different effort than one where you feel pity for these children. When you believe starving children to be in an unfortunate situation, you cast your painful feeling, thoughts, and emotions to the universe to propagate this situation through the principles of creation. Even if you work to help these people as you hold onto the negative feeling, you are not helping to eliminate this situation.

However, once you accept the situation as reality and you see it as something with purpose, you may have compassion to help. Compassion comes from love. In this situation you see starving children and immediately feel love, compassion, and positive emotions. These positive thoughts and emotions set into motion the creation process to bring about positive change to this situation.

Now when you help others by giving money, food, or shelter, you do so with the benefit of the power of your positive energy

SECRETS OF THE MIRACLE INSIDE

which will definitely manifest in helping to change the situation. Some of the change comes from your actions, but most of the change occurs because of your emotions; therefore, it is of utmost importance to have *only* love and compassion behind your actions rather than pity and sorrow for the situation.

Happiness comes from within when you know the secret

Your happiness does not depend upon anything outside of you. Nothing outside of you can alter your happiness unless you believe it can and you allow it. True happiness is created when you learn to see that the world is only perfect all the time, and the way to change it is through your creative power using positive emotions and beliefs. All "negative" situations exist to trigger you to change, so you can see the truth. Those events provide the opportunity to change to see yourself and other people as part of the Source and part of each other.

The negative situations motivate you through the painful feeling you have when you fail to see the truth. Those events keep making you feel bad until you learn to see the truth: that you are outside the illusion. Many people live their entire lives without finding this truth. It is a miracle for those who find this secret. When you do find it — you find yourself in a world without pain, without sadness, without anger, and without fear ever again.

Once you know the secret, there is nothing to fear because nothing can go wrong. Whatever happens, you believe it is supposed to happen and you welcome it as a perfect part of your experience. Even when you would like circumstances to be different, you welcome the change that will shape new beliefs in you or show you a change you must make.

In your new life of knowing the secret you see all people around you as extensions of the Source and parts of you. When people attempt to hurt you, you feel compassion for them because you know they are a part of you. Events that once evoked anger now evoke love, compassion, and hope for others to find the joy you have found.

When you embrace what "is," you don't feel the need to change the world or the way people are; you allow events in your life to be as they are. By doing so you become free — free to be happy, free from anger, free from hurts, free from struggles, free from discomfort, free from anxiety, free from poverty, free from sadness, free to think about love and peace, and free to create powerful emotions of love and project them to the world around you. And when you do that, the world sends it all back to you because the world is the mirror that reflects what is inside of you. This, my friend, is the Secret of the Miracle Inside.

When you see that
events in the world
happen for you
rather than to you,
you find joy in it all.

CHAPTER 10

Transcend the Illusion

This chapter helps you to live in the reality of knowing you are divine while you still live on this earth. This is *Step Ten* of the **Ten Steps to Finding the Secret Inside**.

The Ten Steps to Finding the Secret Inside

1. Understand your current perception
2. Heal your emotional pain
3. Look inside yourself
4. Choose new beliefs
5. Live in the present
6. Find creative power within you
7. Be emotionally aware
8. Align your personality
9. Embrace what "Is"
10. *Transcend the illusion*

Transcending the Mind

Life is full of distractions; life is filled with things to do in order to survive. It is easy to become caught up in the business of living physical lives with no time to experience the reality of who you are, your Source.

> *I had learned about "God" since the day I was born, although the teaching was strict Christianity. And over the course of thirty years I was not able to achieve a state of being one with God or even being close to it until I learned to find "God" inside myself.*

The secret to life is inside you. Inside you is the answer to everything you have ever wanted. Inside you is the knowledge you need in order to find everything you want:

+ Peace
+ Financial freedom
+ Good health
+ Happiness
+ Free time
+ Love

Inside you is the secret of a miracle. Inside you is the space where you find your identity, where you and your Source exist as one. This miracle is the key to eliminating all pain and suffering. Inside you is the key to finding complete everlasting joy and happiness, starting today and lasting forever.

Inside you, in the quiet space between thoughts, is the knowledge that you and your Source are one. You have always known it and now only need to remember it. Inside you is the real *you* waiting to be found. You have always been part of the Source even before creation occurred.

When you were one with the Source, you chose to separate into parts in order to experience each part and to experience all that is contained in the Source. You agreed to forget your own divinity in order to experience pain and misfortune. The Source could never experience that because it cannot be hurt. You had to allow yourself to be veiled from the truth, to live in an illusion for a while in order to gain this experience.

The plan was always for you to experience it only temporarily, and then to remember who you are. When you remember who you are, you find that you are, in fact, the thinking acting part of the Source, now living a human experience. The illusion makes life look difficult, painful, and filled with struggles. Once outside of the illusion, you see that the world is wonderful, filled with peace and full of love.

All the people in the world are parts of the Source. You and everyone else once knew who you were and agreed to give up the memory of your deity in order to undergo these experiences. You knew you could not really get hurt, nor could anyone else. You knew it was only an illusion of real pain, and still you wanted to acquire that knowledge.

Now, when you feel hurt, you understand that this is impossible while knowing the truth. In order to feel bad you must not be seeing the truth. This is living in the illusion. You only think you hurt. You see that everyone is living the experience that they chose as part of the Source. All people are living according to their own beliefs and all are setting into motion the future of their own lives.

You have the ability to step outside of the illusion at any time and see the way things really are. Today you have the choice to never step back into the illusion. Today you can choose to live as the divine being you are and keep the memory of who you were. You have the choice to operate on a higher level than those in the illusion. You have the choice to create your own future, to create happiness, to create wealth, to create the world that you want. You have the ability to look at everything in the world and see it as perfect and good because it is the great learning ground for the Source to grow.

In the middle of death, pain, suffering, hunger and poverty, the Source that created everything is alive and well. The Source chooses to live the lives of people like you and me. Pain exists only when you believe the false illusion that you are separate from your Source. You are not separate; the pain is not real; it only feels real when you believe the illusion. If you are tired of that feeling and want to move back to being perfect and happy all the time, then do it by changing your belief! You are part of the divine Source.

The Source can choose to live in pleasure and happiness just as easily as choosing to experience fear, pain, and suffering. Much of this world is living in the illusion of disconnection with the Source. This is not bad; this is perfect. This is what you planned to do for a while too. It is also part of your plan that you awaken to see who you are. You can realize who you are if you choose to acknowledge it. Part of the illusion was to forget who you are. Even when others try to tell you, you might refuse to believe it. Parts of the Source all over the world refuse to believe who they are; they refuse to recognize their own identity, their own power, their own divinity.

To transcend the physical world means to rise above it or to operate on a level of consciousness where the pain of the world is not seen as pain. Transcending means you live in this world while your mind and spirit are operating in the realm of the divine. Transcending means you know you are part of the Source. You know you are not separate from the Source. You know nothing can hurt you unless you choose to let it hurt you.

This is how you are able to forgive and love those who try to hurt you. This is how you cannot be hurt and are able to be peaceful at all times.

Remember who you are. The world has many distractions that tempt you to forget who you are. Everyone around you believes that you and they are separate from their Source. They tempt you to believe you are separate too. If you believe that, you will begin to experience the pain as they do. But if you never forget who you are, you will remain at peace.

While living in this busy life where it is so easy to become distracted, take time each day to relax and go inside yourself to the quiet place without thoughts, and remember who you are. Remind yourself that the details of your life are part of the plan that you created before you were born. Meditate on the fact that you are a part of your Source who has lived from before the beginning of time and will live into eternity. Along the way you continue to improve and evolve — forever. You do this by living many lives and gaining new experiences. In some of those lives, you forget who you are. When you do, life becomes painful. Right now, in this life, you are blessed if you have awakened to see the illusion and the reality of who you truly are.

Meditate about the purpose of your life and what it is that you are here to accomplish. Be certain you are not thinking about the details of your career or the "stuff" of your life. Find your purpose and put into practice the principles of creation to direct your life to become whatever it is you desire. Then when the problems of life arise, you will not take life too seriously because you know none of those details matter. What matters is not what happens physically, but what is happening in your thoughts and emotions. This is where everything is created. Physical life is the manifestation of everything first thought of in the mind of the Source.

Transcend Pain and Suffering

You have learned that pain and suffering can be felt only by the false sense of self when you are in the illusion. When emotional pain and suffering are felt, the way to transcend them is to meditate and remember who you are. Review the facts of your origin. Meditate on the knowledge within yourself that confirms you are from ancient times and you have divine power to overcome pain and suffering.

Jesus said, "My people perish for lack of knowledge." It is the knowledge of understanding who you are that gives you the power to overcome suffering. Part of that knowledge is to know the steps that must occur in order to remove the suffering.

1. Meditate upon the knowledge of who you are and the power within you to become love, peace, and joy.

2. Be emotionally aware and sensitive to what you are feeling. The feelings might be pain, suffering, anger, or sorrow. Before you were born you chose to experience these feeling.

Once you have the experience, you can choose immediately to regain peace. If you forget who you are and get stuck in the illusion, your own pain is there to remind you to get unstuck.

3.   The hurt and pain are there to remind you that you are now operating in the realm of the illusion of a person separated from your Source. Meditate to remind yourself that you are part of the divine Source.

4.   Listen to the message of the emotions. Do not think about the details or the action that have brought about an emotion. The details are always changing and have nothing to do with the message. The emotion is most likely a familiar one to you. The feeling might be one of sorrow, fear, anger, or self pity. Feel the emotion and recognize how it is familiar to you.

5.   Once you recognize the emotion, think about the belief that is necessary for this emotion to exist. It might be fear of not being loved, fear of unworthiness, fear of no control, fear that God is not helping, fear that things will go wrong, or something else. You must find the belief that is causing this hurt to exist.

6.   When you find that belief, state the opposite. For example, assume the belief is that something can go wrong. Because of that you feel anxious and fearful about some aspect of life. The opposite of that belief is affirming that nothing can go wrong because all things are happening exactly according to your own divine plan.

7.   Think about what emotions you would have if you believed

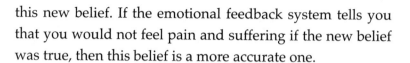

this new belief. If the emotional feedback system tells you that you would not feel pain and suffering if the new belief was true, then this belief is a more accurate one.

8. Choose to accept this belief. The entire purpose of your pain and suffering is to get your attention and to show you the error in your belief and to show you a better belief in order to get out of being stuck in the illusion that you are separate from your Source.

9. Meditate on the new belief and affirm it.

10. Recall the emotions of pain that initiated this process. Thank them for coming to show you a new and better belief. Tell them goodbye and make the bad feelings pass out of you. Acknowledge that their purpose has now been fulfilled.

11. Remember that you are divine, and recognize that you have just performed a miracle. You have tapped into the consciousness of the Source and received divine guidance. Most astonishing is the fact that you are this divine being. You are the Source of this information because you are a part of the universal consciousness from which all things originate.

12. The life circumstances that brought about this emotion are not important. What is important is the message and end result to fulfill your perfect plan to experience life and remember your own divinity.

Experience What You Already Are — Divine

Your desire should be simply what you already are. You are

a spiritual being who has taken on the form of a human being for this life journey. Knowing that you are a spirit who has lived before and who will continue to live for eternity should cause you to want to act like the divine being you are.

While you lived in the illusion of believing you were separate from your Source, you got the chance to experience a life of pain and suffering. You paid your dues and fulfilled the plan you had designed for yourself to experience. Now that you are awakened, strive to regain the memory of your divinity and the power you have.

During meditation, train your mind to care no longer about what you will do tomorrow or what you will wear or what you will eat. Don't worry about the money you will make or the money you will lose or the work day you must face soon. Don't be concerned about the work problems you must solve or the challenges you will face each day.

At this moment in meditation, know who you are. You do not exist without the Source, and the Source does not exist without you. You are one with it and you are one with all the other people on the earth. You are one with the animals, the trees, the plants and the rocks.

The difficult people in your life are the Source coming to you in disguise. They are part of *you* being manifest as another person. While you know you are divine, you cannot experience the hurt. The only way to experience it is to agree to be born without remembering your divinity. You are born into the illusion, believing you are separate from the divine Source.

This gives you the only way to experience pain and suffering. Apparently, at one time you wanted to experience this or else you would not be experiencing it. The system has a built-in mechanism to wake you up to the truth. That mechanism is the pain that results from believing you are separate from the Source. That pain prompts you to look within and find the *secret of the miracle*, it tells you who you are. You gave yourself the tools to get yourself out of the illusion of the pain. Once outside you do not need to ever step back into it. You can live pain-free, sorrow-free, and burden-free for the rest of eternity. You can experience only what you want to experience.

Living in Spirit

When you learn to connect with the Source, you find another world, one filled with peace and happiness everywhere. While learning to experience this new world, you find yourself bouncing back and forth between that wonderful world of peace and the world you grew up in, that of real life, work, family, and struggles. If you do not meditate often, you begin to feel as if reality is the physical world with all its hardships. It might seem that meditation is a psychological way to escape the difficulties and imagine a better life. When you do not meditate often, the duties of physical life become most real and your meditation sessions may appear only as an escape mode.

However, if you meditate often, it appears the opposite is true. It seems that reality is living outside the illusion, living in total peace and happiness all the time. Outside the illusion you see the physical world as a mechanism to allow spiritual activity to be manifest.

The difference between the perspectives of living in the illusion of being separate from your Source compared to the perspective of being part of your Source is similar to how you view being physically awake compared to being asleep and dreaming. When you are awake, you think of your dreams as not real, but when you dream you think of them as real. When you are awake you call your awake-time the real experience. While awake you recognize your dreams as imaginations in your mind. Yet in the moment of dreaming, the dream seems to be real. In your dreams you cannot distinguish the dream from the non-dream. At that moment it is real in every way — the hurt, the sadness, the fear, the happiness, and the love.

> *I learned at a young age to be night-time potty trained. Yet, even as an older child, I sometimes had an accidental bed wetting. One time when I wet my bed, it occurred while I dreamed I was on the toilet. In my dream at that moment I was on the toilet but I suddenly felt a warm sensation and, within a few seconds, awoke to realize I had just wet my bed.*
>
> *I realized that sitting on the toilet was in my dream and in reality I had been sleeping and wet my bed. Several days or weeks later, I found myself needing to go to the toilet and recalled the recent dream. I wanted to be sure that I did not wet my bed again. Before I sat down on the toilet, I pounded my fist on my chest a few times to make sure I felt real pain, to be sure I was wide awake, and that this was not another dream.*
>
> *This time, I knew I was awake. When you are really awake you know it. I knew I was awake this time. So I knew it was all right to sit down on the toilet and go. As soon as I did, I felt a warm sensation below my waist and within a few seconds I awoke to find myself wetting the bed again. Despite my attempts to ensure that I was awake, the dream had fooled me again.*

You cannot distinguish your dreams from your reality. Wherever your mind is at the moment, is where you will perceive reality to be. When you are dreaming, you will perceive the dream to be reality. Yet when you are awake you perceive that to be reality.

Right now you believe the act of reading this book is *reality* because this is the state you are in at this moment. You will always feel reality is where your mind is at that moment in time, just as I did in my dream before I wet my bed. But how do you know for certain? Can you ever know for certain? When you meditate you feel as though your spiritual connection to the universe is the stronger reality. Your dreams show you another reality. The truth is you cannot distinguish one reality from another.

Choose Your Reality

You must choose which reality you want for your life: the one inside the illusion or the one outside the illusion. By choosing your reality you choose the entire outcome of your life, your happiness, your connection to your Source and your future, both in life and in death.

The reality inside the illusion where you believe you are separate from your Source provides an experience of discontent, hard work, and circumstances that you don't like. People hurt you, money is scarce, relationships are stressful, and you are a slave to your job for the rest of your life.

Life brings struggles, hurt and pain. You feel anger and fear instead of the love you want to feel. Moreover, what you see happening in the world involves war, sickness, loss, disappointment, violence, power struggles, death, crime, and hopelessness. In this reality there seems to be nothing good in this life. The best outlook is to hope that after death things get better.

The other reality is to believe that you and the Source are one, providing an experience to make miracles, create your own future, find love, produce happiness, create good health, make all the money you want and see that everything happening in the world is perfect just the way it is, and that you are always peaceful and overflowing with joy.

You create every moment of your life through the thoughts and beliefs you choose. You can create the details for the rest of your life right now. Do you choose illusion or the reality of the Secrets of the Miracle Inside?

We hope you enjoyed this book.
If you'd like to review more articles
and upcoming books by this author,
visit our websites at:

www.TheSecretsInside.com

MIRACLE WRITERS, LLC
PUBLISHING COMPANY

RCM #28550

P.O. Box 4120

Portland, OR 98208-4120

USA

www.MiracleWriters.com

Author's Note

The writing of this book was inspired by the Source that created the universe, and that created me and lives within me. The Source is the energy which brings forth imagination within me along with the perseverance necessary to make those imaginations become reality.

The Source must not be viewed as anything separate from me; otherwise, I might wait forever to hear a guiding voice which does not come. I must believe without seeing that the Source is within me, and I must choose to initiate action toward my goal.

Yet, once I initiate action, the energy of the Source takes hold of me and directs me as though I am only a conduit for the Source to manifest whatever it is the Source wishes. That is how this book became written. The ideas and words flowed through me with ease when I believed and then allowed it to be written.

About the Author

Early in life, Paul McCormick found the ability to achieve success in whatever it was that he desired, or so he thought.

He became a corporation partner at age twenty-seven and CEO at age twenty-nine. Despite his career success, wonderful family, and his strong faith, he knew something was still missing. As he searched desperately to find it, his life only got worse. Eventually, he felt depressed to the point he wanted life to end.

Then a miracle happened. He found the secret inside himself. His transformation was so great, it changed his life forever. He resigned his position as CEO, and now writes and speaks about the secret that can change your life forever.

DATE DUE

			PRINTED IN U.S.A.